A Voice For Ira

Dale Ross

Published by Dale Ross, 2022.

While every precaution has been taken in the preparation of this book, the publisher assumes no responsibility for errors or omissions, or for damages resulting from the use of the information contained herein.

A VOICE FOR IRA

First edition. August 18, 2022.

Copyright © 2022 Dale Ross.

ISBN: 979-8215978658

Written by Dale Ross.

Table of Contents

FOREWORD

I think a majority of us still tend to favor the underdog against the giant. We prefer truth and honesty over half-truths and dishonesty. When someone is victimized and does not have a voice in their circumstances, we feel an outrage for the injustice. Upon reading the story of how Ira Gurley died in a horrible accident inside the State Capital Building, red lights began flashing inside my head. The story is tragic, and even plausible, until you weigh in all of the surrounding circumstances. Then all of the unanswered questions start to pop up, and you can't imagine how this event could have happened without someone being accountable. Maybe this was a horrific accident, and maybe it was something else, but 90 years later, we can only look at the facts we know, and wonder why so many questions were left unanswered. To best visualize this event, you have to understand the era. 1932 Depression Era Arkansas was nothing like today. Times were hard and the people that survived were harder.

Put yourself into 1932 Depression Era Arkansas. You've decided to make a run for the office of Secretary of State, and you have four terms of serving in the Arkansas House of Representatives under your belt. You travel to the Arkansas State Capital building for a meeting, and while leaving the building, you are crushed in the door frame of an elevator, by one of the current Secretary of State employees. No Law Enforcement Agency is called! Instead, the Secretary of State himself will handle the investigation of how you died! We're told the man operating the elevator is the Assistant Elevator Operator, but is he? We're told one of your co-workers is going to witness the investigation, but is that the real reason he is there?

What a strange and unbelievable nightmare this sounds like. Could it have actually happened to someone? This may be the easiest question in this whole book to answer, because, yes it happened, and we know it happened, but do we really know the details of what happened?

Ira Gurley was sitting on the Arkansas Game & Fish Commission in 1932. He had served four terms as a member of the House of Representatives from Green Forest, Arkansas in Carroll County. He had let it be known of his plans to run for Secretary of State, and was at the State Capital building attending a meeting. As he left the meeting, a terrible accident awaited him in the elevator on the third floor. The man operating the elevator said he never saw or heard Ira until it was too late to save him. A man that we're told was the Assistant Elevator Operator, but a real investigation could have easily proven his real job. He was a janitor. The same man that as soon as the accident was over, was told to leave and let the Secretary of State handle the investigation and talking to the media. The man operating the elevator that day was never interrogated.

Why didn't the Secretary of State admit the obvious appearance of impropriety and step aside? Why was it so important to him that no law enforcement agency be involved? Why was the elevator operator immediately sent home? Why did two ladies that had just gotten off of the elevator see and hear nothing? The same two ladies that stated Ira was standing right in front of the elevator doors when they opened. Both ladies saw him, but for some reason, the man running the elevator didn't.

Even if everything we've been told about this accident is true, Ira Gurley deserved better. He deserved to have the accident investigated by trained law enforcement. He deserved to have the witnesses separated and interrogated. But ninety years later is too late for that, so all we can do is finally put the facts into order, and let each reader make up their own mind if everything seems to have been on the up and up, or perhaps, does the whole affair scream of a cover up?

Nobody in this book is accused of doing anything other than a shoddy investigation and playing loose with the whole truth. Half truths and Political speak, without telling the public everything, seems to be accepted as fact in this case. But Ira deserves the whole truth to be told, and hopefully this book accomplishes just that. Please keep in mind as you read, that the time was 1932. The Era of the Great Depression, Mobsters, and One Party Rule in Arkansas.

CHAPTER ONE
GIVING VOICE TO IRA GURLEY

Was Ira Gurley the victim of foul play? It's a fair question when you consider all of the questions left unanswered after his death. It's been ninety years since the tragic day in the Arkansas State Capital building when Ira was crushed in the door frame of an elevator. The purpose of this book is to simply try and reconstruct the events of that day, and to learn as much as possible about the characters involved. Ira will always have a place in history, not only for his accomplishments, but for also being the father of Helen Gurley Brown, the famous author and long time Editor-In-Chief of Cosmopolitan Magazine.

We'll look back at the life of Ira Gurley and his upbringing in the Arkansas Ozark Mountains, along with his teaching, administrative, and law career. Ira was a family man, his wife and daughters destiny after the tragedy will be explored.

It's also relevant to examine the times and politics of the era. It was 1932 and the country was in a devastating National Economic Depression. Arkansas politics was dominated by the Democrat Party. The 1930's also brought the Era of the Gangsters, which made Hot Springs, Arkansas a playground and safe haven for criminals.

We will look at the statements of witnesses and participants, so that the reader can determine for themselves the likelihood of truth. When all the facts are laid out, then like myself, you'll be left with lots of questions and asking yourself, "was there a cover up in the investigation"? Could there have been foul play involved? Why wasn't the Law Enforcement officers asked to investigate?

I want to make it clear, early and often, that I am not accusing anyone of murder. I do not have proof of a murder, and ninety years after the death, I cannot attain proof. There is nobody to interrogate, no crime scene to examine, and no witnesses to interview. We are left with the story we were told. What I can do, is look at the story we were told and take it apart piece by piece, and see if what we were told makes sense. I've spent many months studying this story, and every time I learn something new, it brings up new questions about what happened that day in 1932. The story just falls short of an explanation, and what was done after the accident screams that something is being hidden. For the first time ever, someone is speaking up for Ira Gurley. I wish someone had done so in 1932, but here's a book giving Ira a voice in this investigation, and what we know today.

The Secretary of State, Ed F. McDonald, spoke for the investigation, his office, and employees, but who was there speaking for Ira Gurley? Nobody! And of course, Ira couldn't speak for himself. So this whole story we got explaining how the accident happened is one sided. We got the Secretary of State, Ed F. McDonald story, we got the Assistant Elevator Operators story, and we got the findings of the Coroner. We did not get any investigation that might give us the Ira Gurley story. He has laid quietly in his grave for ninety years now, unable to tell his side of the story. It's time Ira had a voice and all the details of this investigation are exposed, and maybe we'll all have the feeling a different scenario may have unfolded that day.

CHAPTER TWO
WHY WRITE THIS BOOK NOW?

I sit on the Board of Directors for the Carroll County Arkansas Historical and Genealogy Society. I've been a Board Member and Officer of the Board for the past five years. I've researched thousands of past stories and artifacts over the years, but none left me with the same unanswered questions that this story left me with. Maybe my years of service with the Sherwood Police Department, or maybe just a curious nature by birth, kept driving me to look for explanations of what happened that summer day in June of 1932. I couldn't believe that I couldn't find more books or articles where some smart investigative reporter dug into the accident to get answers. But I couldn't find anything other than the newspaper articles of 1932 that described the accident as told to them by Secretary of State Ed McDonald. I couldn't get a police report, because no police department investigated the accident. I couldn't get a copy of the Coroners report, because if one was ever written, it is now lost to time. The Secretary of State wrote no reports on the accident. I received nothing about the accident from the Arkansas State Archives. Newspaper archives from 1932, with all telling the same story, were the only available resource. So what was a man to do if he wanted answers? The only thing I know to do is just print out in order what happened that day and let everyone make up their own mind if the story told is plausible. There are many coincidences and odd facts to this story that probably couldn't be replicated in a million years.

I've visited the burial site of Ira Gurley and stood beside his grave in Green Forest, Arkansas. His life was taken away at a far too early age, and his accomplishments so early in life should not be so easily forgotten. Nobody speaks about Ira Gurley today, no observances are held at his graveside, and there's no statues or memorials constructed in Ira's honor. His family is buried in Osage, Arkansas just a few miles south of where Ira lies in rest. He lost so much that day in 1932, and after ninety years, I think it's time someone asked for him....why?

I only have the story told at the time of his death. I have no new evidence, reports, or admissions of guilt to uncover. I only have the ability to list all of the facts and let everyone else judge the credibility of what supposedly happened. Ninety years after the fact, I can prove no wrong doing or evil intent. But, I believe I can show plainly that a cover up was plotted and used. And a cover up usually points to one thing, and that's that there's something that certain people would prefer to keep secret and not become public knowledge. But what?

When, at the time you have finished reading this book, you feel that it's obvious that this was a terrible accident and I'm just some crazy conspiracy theorist, then I have failed to explain my point. But if you read this book and agree with me that everything is not on the up and up in this story, then I've successfully accomplished the awakening to the facts that have for so many years lay dormant. Either way you decide, at least you will have a fundamental knowledge of who Ira Gurley was and what a shame it is that we lost this bright mind at such a crucial time in Arkansas and Carroll County history.

Long after this book is published, I'll still be going about my business of preserving history for the people of Carroll County.

There will be no rewriting of history books, because no writing of this story has been told. But I'll feel that I've done my duty to Ira Gurley and his family by finally being that one person, or voice, that asked why, and questioned the facts of the official story. Why question the story? Because there are holes all over this story from beginning to end. Large holes that just do no make sense or add up. When you know all of the facts associated with this accident, accepting the story as told is not acceptable. There's more answers that need to be told, but ninety years after the fact, we'll never get the answers. But accepting all of this does not keep us from questioning the story and making our own minds up as to what probably happened that day. So, Lets look at what we were told, and we'll start to break it all down from there. Hang on to your seats, because your not going to believe all of this happened in the State Capital building of Arkansas.

CHAPTER THREE
THE ACCIDENT

It was during the lunch hour on June 17th, 1932. A man, Ira Gurley, stood on the third floor of the Arkansas State Capital building waiting for the elevator. In 1932 elevators were not automatic, they had human operators. The elevator arrived on the third floor and the outer doors opened, and the operator opened the cage door that slid from side to side allowing two ladies to get off. The elevator operator, Albert Sanders, would have known that there was a passenger waiting by the light display and ringing in the elevator telling him someone was on the third floor and had summoned the elevator. As the two ladies stepped off the elevator, Ira Gurley had to step to the side to allow them to pass. Described by witness's as almost instantly, without closing the elevator doors, Mr. Sanders started the elevator upward. As the two women passed Ira, he attempted to hop onto the moving elevator. Albert Sanders stated that he did not see Mr. Gurley as he slid the door closed, pinning Ira in the doorway as the elevator was rising. Ira had his head and feet inside the elevator, but his back was outside. Mr. Sanders stated that by the time he realized that he had pinned Ira in the doorway, it was too late to stop the elevator. Ira was crushed between the elevator floor and the upper door frame. Albert Sanders then stopped the elevator and pulled Ira inside. He next took the elevator to the basement where he notified his employer, Secretary of State Ed McDonald. Mr. McDonald later stated that an ambulance was immediately called and arrived within minutes.

Ira Gurley was pronounced dead by the ambulance crew before arriving at the hospital.

Hiring in the Arkansas State Capital is done through the Secretary of State office. This includes maintenance, housekeeping, gift shop employees, yard and gardening, and anything else needed to maintain the building, such as elevator operators. Today, the Secretary of State office also employs the Capital Police Department, which has jurisdiction over the Capital and grounds around the Capital Complex. But in 1932 the Capital Police Department did not exist.

Since there was no Police Department with immediate jurisdiction in the Capital, it certainly would have been proper, (and probably expected), if Ed McDonald had asked a law enforcement agency to step in and investigate the accident. The Arkansas State Police did not become an agency until 1935, but the Little Rock Police Department and the Pulaski County Sheriff's Department were available. After all, this was one of Mr. McDonalds employees, and to avoid an appearance of impropriety, it would have been proper procedure to hand the investigation over to an outside agency. It makes even more sense when you factor in that Ira Gurley had let it be known he was running for the Secretary of State office, which was held by Mr. McDonald. But Ed McDonald chose not to invite in a certified trained investigation team. The steps he takes next, in the opinion of this author, borders on cover up.

According to Ed McDonald, he went to the basement and interviewed Albert Sanders. In no part of the story does Ed McDonald question Albert Sanders as to why he started the elevator with the doors open. He simply said he didn't see anyone and started the elevator up as soon as the two women had stepped out. He slid the interior cage door closed and Mr. Gurley, trying to jump onto the elevator, was pinned and crushed. Ed McDonald said Albert Sanders looked so upset about what he had done, that Mr. McDonald was afraid he might collapse. So out of worry for poor Mr. Sanders, he was sent home! No record of this interview can be found, since no certified investigator was present. We're just suppose to take Mr. McDonald's word for it. This is hard to believe that it happened, Albert crushed a man to death in the door of an elevator, and got sent home to rest. Any more questions from this point on would be handled by Ed McDonald, and handle it he did.

The next step in Ed McDonald's investigation, (I'm having trouble calling it an investigation), also brings up more questions. Ed McDonald did not want to call in a police agency, but his fellow elected Democrat friend, Dr. Samuel Boyce was called in to legitimize the findings. Dr. Boyce was the Pulaski County Coroner. The Secretary of State needed someone that could officially declare the death an accident. According to the mission of the Coroners office, they are: to accurately determine the manner and cause of death of individuals that die within the statutory jurisdiction of Pulaski County, through a fair, ethical, and competent investigation of death, performed by qualified and trained individuals, in accordance with the accepted medicolegal death investigation professional standards, ensuring the integrity of the investigation.

Dr. Boyce was assisted in the investigation by Guy Amsler, Secretary of the Arkansas Game and Fish Commission, which Ira Gurley also sat on. What were Mr. Amsler credentials to investigate a death? It's stated to give the impression that one of Ira Gurley's friends and co-worker was there to investigate his death, but what they don't tell you, is that Guy Amsler was an attorney. Not just any attorney, but one that represented the State in law suits. So it may have sounded like one of Ira's friends was there to help with the investigation, but in fact he was an attorney that was most likely advising Ed McDonald on what to say and what not to say. But none of this is documented. So, according to the newspaper accounts of the accident, Dr. Boyce and Mr. Amsler were told what happened by Mr. McDonald. We have to remember that the man that was running the elevator had already been sent home. The two investigators then talked to the ladies that had just gotten off of the elevator. Both agreed that the elevator started immediately after they stepped off, but neither heard or saw anything after Mr. Gurley had stepped past them. After speaking to Ed McDonald and the two ladies, Dr. Boyce declared the death officially an accidental death. No mention of negligent homicide was ever made. No reason for Mr. Sanders starting the elevator with the doors open was ever given. Dr. Boyce never spoke to Albert Sanders. He simply heard the story given to him, and signed off on it as official. I included the mission of the Coroner office so you can determine for yourself if Dr. Boyce "accurately determined the manner and cause of death through a fair, ethical, and competent investigation."

I spoke to the Pulaski County Coroner office and asked if a Coroners Report might still be on file in their office. They were willing to look, but needed a few days to search. When I contacted them again, I was told that a file box marked 1932 does exist, but there's nothing about Ira Gurley in the file. No report, and no record. I do not understand how that could be possible, but nobody that was a part of this incident wanted to leave a paper trail. If they had told me that they don't keep records back that far, I would have understood. But the fact that they had a box containing records from 1932, but Ira Gurley was not in it, just caused more questions that can't be answered.

By the time I had gotten this far into the investigation, I was determined that a book needed to be written. Ira Gurley needed a voice, and his story needed to be told. The people of Arkansas need to know who Ira was, and hopefully not just be a forgotten victim of his times. So let's take a look at all of the characters in this incident, and try to answer questions so that we can determine for ourselves if accidental death is likely, or was there something else, something much more involved, going on in the Arkansas State Capital that June day.

CHAPTER FOUR
IRA GURLEY

The main character, and reason for this book, is the victim in this tragedy, Ira Gurley. We'll debate if he was the victim of a horrendous accident, or a victim of something else entirely, but in either scenario he was a victim.

Ira was born in the county border town of Alpena, Arkansas on October 10, 1891. Alpena sits on the border of Carroll and Boone Counties in Northwest Arkansas on the route of Highway 62. The town was also sometimes called Alpena Pass when the railroad came through in 1901. As a historical sidenote, for a short period of time before moving to Eureka Springs, Arkansas, the famous suffragette Carrie A. Nation lived in Alpena.

Ira grew up in the area of Alpena and fell in love with a local girl from Osage, Arkansas named Cleo Fred Sisco in 1917. Both Ira and Cleo were school teachers, and knew the importance of education for not only themselves, but the local children of Carroll County. Two words that seem to describe Ira Gurley would be ambitious and self-motivated. He understood early in life that the secret to success for a young man from a poor farming community was education. Ira was the role model that a good education and hard work could provide him and his family with prosperity. He was never shy about taking a position of leadership. Teaching in several schools in the area, both Ira and Cleo taught school at Green Forest, Arkansas. Ira also served as Principal for a time at Green Forest and Alpena. The young couple had two daughters, Mary, born in 1917, and Helen, born in 1922 in Green Forest.

Showing the same traits that described her father, Helen would later become a famous author, publisher, business woman, and Editor-In-Chief of Cosmopolitan Magazine for 32 years.

Ira had graduated from Green Forest High School and was certainly well respected enough to run for the Arkansas House of Representatives without a law degree. But, Ira knew to gain the respect of the rest of the State of Arkansas as a law maker, a law degree would be a great asset to his future. He attained his Law Degree in 1917 from Cumberland Law School in Lebanon, Tennessee. With a degree attained, Ira was ready to start focusing on his political plans. He was a man with a bright outlook and had the encouragement of his community.

Ira Gurley while serving in the Arkansas House Of
Representatives

IRA AND FAMILY WERE members of the Methodist Church in
Green Forest and he served as superintendent of the Sunday School
for several years. Ira and Cleo both taught Sunday School classes
in the Church. Ira was also a member of the Modern Woodmen
of America. Although still a young man, Ira had the education and
willingness to serve his community, and he became a respected role
model that led by example.

In the Arkansas elections of 1918, Ira Gurley was elected by his community to be their State Representative in the Arkansas House of Representatives. He was re-elected in 1920, 22, and 24. During his last three terms in office, he was Chief Clerk of the House of Representatives. In 1925 Ira was appointed by the Governor as an Assistant Secretary Commissioner to the Arkansas Game & Fish Commission. He still held that position at the time of his death. He also had let his intentions to run for the office of Secretary of State be known. Ira was a rising star in Arkansas politics.

Some men are born as natural leaders, and all indications and writings about Ira Gurley tell us he was one of those men. If it was in his schools, church, or community, Ira took a position of leadership. His personality and demeanor impressed his peers, that trusted him with the education of their children, the teaching of faith in their Church, and as their Representative in the State Capital. Would Ira have become Arkansas Secretary of State? Would Ira have gone on to attain even higher office? We'll never know, but if the tragic incident in the State Capital building had not happened, my money would have been on Ira to achieve whatever goal he set out to attain.

After being elected to four terms in the Arkansas House of Representatives, and spending six years as the Chief Clerk of the House, Ira had gained the attention of more than just Carroll County. The State of Arkansas knew who Ira Gurley was, and he was a rising name in politics as the Country was falling deeper into a National Depression. Voters were looking for leaders with uncanny abilities to help them find a way out of the economic disaster that had a grasp on the Nation. A young, handsome, educated over-achiever from a rural county would have been an attractive candidate for many voters in the State. This was good news for Ira, but it could also make him a feared option by some that already held elected office. Times were hard, and nobody wanted to lose their job.

CHAPTER FIVE
1930'S POLITICAL LANDSCAPE

In the 1930's, Arkansas was a poor rural state for the most part, and this was certainly true for Carroll County. The state had a very small Republican organization, but the Democrat Party controlled the political landscape of Arkansas. It was "a one party state" that left voters little choice once the primaries were over. This meant that the Governor, Lt. Governor, Secretary of State, Attorney General, State Treasurer, State Auditor, Mayors, Sheriffs, Coroners, Justice of the Peace, and every other elected official were, for the most part, all part of one political party. In a political system that has no checks and balances, the chances of corruption and turning a blind eye to corruption is almost a guarantee. This can be said for either Political Party, because one Party rule breeds a political atmosphere that is ripe for corruption and dirty dealing. With this in mind, lets look at other factors of the times in Arkansas.

When the events of this book occurred, the entire country was in the clutches of The Great Depression. The economy had fallen and jobs were hard to find. The perils of Arkies trying to find work has been well documented in the classic epics such as "The Grapes of Wrath" by John Steinbeck. The common man didn't have the time, nor the inclination to pay attention to political affairs. What was important to them was finding ways to feed their family. It was widely believed that Herbert Hoover, a Republican, had caused this Great Depression, and their local politicians were doing everything possible to correct the calamity of the country. The

Depression helped to solidify the Democrat Party and entrench them in public office. It was preached from the pulpits that Republicans were "only for the rich" and Democrats were for the "every day working man". If you dared to walk into a polling booth and voted for a Republican, it would surely mean doom and gloom on the poor working families. This ideology became so entrenched into the mindset of the population, that it still persist even today. So, with the welfare of their friends and families at stake, the voters of Arkansas did their civic duty for the common man and elected only one Party to serve their State.

Now, lets take a look at a group of people that did have plenty of money and influence in the State of Arkansas during the 1930's. To keep it simple, The Mobsters. Perhaps when you think of big crime bosses and their like, you think of places like New York, New Jersey, Chicago, or Las Vegas. All of these locations are certainly known for mob activity during this era. Not everyone knows that the Mob had a playground where they could drink, gamble, and socialize with prostitutes without fear of being arrested by the local authorities. That place was Hot Springs, Arkansas. A place where they could stay at luxury hotels, soak in the bath houses, and gamble the night away. They were generous with their money and as long as the right people were getting their share, the mobsters had no worries, and could relax in Hot Springs until time to head back to the home city. The mobsters soon ran the casino's, hotels, and brothels. Let's look at who some of these mobsters were.

Long before Las Vegas became the underworlds casino playground, Hot Springs, Arkansas was home away from home for the most notorious names in organized crime. The list reads like a Who's Who in the world of organized crime. Al Capone, Albert Anastasia, Lucky Luciano, Bugsy Siegel, and Carlos Marcello were just a few that vacationed in Hot Springs. Prostitution and gambling were illegal, but prospered in the open, until shut down in the late 1960's. And it's not surprising that the illegal gaming came to an end when Arkansas elected a Republican, Winthrop Rockefeller, as Governor. The first Republican Governor elected since Reconstruction after the Civil War. With Rockefeller in office, one party could not just wink and turn a head to corruption, and Rockefeller had every Democrat eye in the State of Arkansas on him. For the first time in decades, Arkansas had a system of checks and balances with one Party keeping an eye on the other Party. But this was not the case in 1932.

A couple of stories that have circulated in the media and internet tell how a New York detective on assignment spotted Lucky Luciano walking down Bath House Row in Hot Springs with the local Chief of Detectives. The New York Detective identified himself to Luciano and invited him to return to New York with him, where Luciano would have been arrested. Luciano just smiled and refused the offer, stating he was having too much fun with his friends in Arkansas. Luciano knew he had little to worry about in Hot Springs. According to The Legends of Arkansas website, Hot Springs Mayor Leo McLaughlin reigned as the undisputed boss of Garland County politics. However, McLaughlin took it to a new level using voter fraud and other unlawful tactics to drive his political machine. During his tenure, local law enforcement was controlled by a political machine, and a former sheriff attempted to have the State's anti-gambling laws enforced and to secure honest elections. But this man was murdered in 1937, and no one was ever charged with his killing.

Another story involved Al Capone, who had made Hot Springs one of his preferred getaways. He would rent out entire floors of

Hot Springs hotels, like the Arlington Hotel, for himself and his entourage. The political and legal corruption of Arkansas made Hot Springs a gamblers paradise long before Las Vegas made its mark on the gaming world.

All of this isn't intended to suggest that every politician in Arkansas was corrupt and on the take. Arkansas had its share of good honest men and women that were loyal to their constituents. But the system they worked in was corrupt, and a lot of good men looked the other way when certain activities were going on in the State. An honest man like Ira Gurley, coming from a humble background, just would not suit the lifestyles of these men running the corruption in the State politics. There gangsters of organized crime had their own set of values and loyalties. They were the type of men that, if you did them a favor, they'd do you a favor.

Al Capone

Lucky Luciano

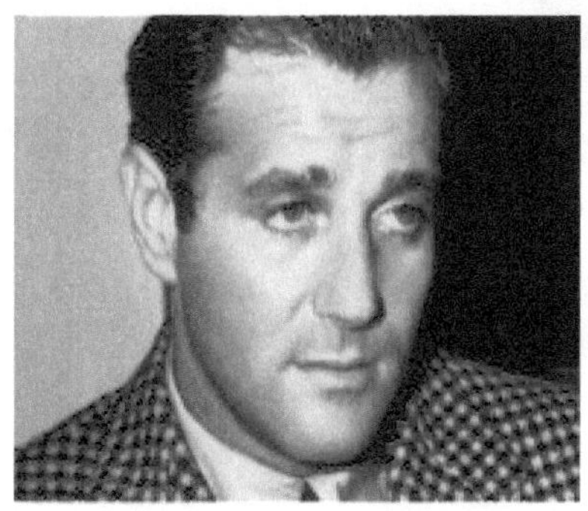

Bugsy Siegel

WHAT OTHER ACTIVITIES tell us about the era? Lets talk about a few well known figures that were in Arkansas during these times.

MAXINE TEMPLE JONES
1915-1997

Maxine Temple Jones was a Hot Springs businesswoman. A well known Madam, with numerous political connections, she managed a lucrative brothel operation that catered to politicians, businessmen, and mobsters. She documented her life in an autobiography published in 1983 titled "Maxine Call Me Madam" the life and times of a Hot Springs Madam. Her business was operating from a house on Palm Street in Hot Springs that came to be known as the Mansion.

THE BARROW GANG
AKA BONNIE & CLYDE

ARKANSAS HAD SEVERAL visits from the Barrow Gang between 1932 and 1934. Their exploits in crime while in Arkansas included murder, attempted murder, kidnapping, robbery, and car theft. A totally different kind of outlaw compared to the big mob bosses, it's been said that the biggest difference was the pay-offs. Perhaps if Bonnie & Clyde had paid the right individuals, a blind eye would have been turned for them also. It sure worked for Al Capone.

PRETTY BOY FLOYD

In the early 1930's, Pretty Boy Floyd, whose actual name was Charles Floyd, visited northwest Arkansas many times. To the poor residence of this area, Floyd was like a modern day Robin Hood, buying groceries and giving money to people down on their luck. But this activity masked a far darker side of Floyd, whose criminal rampage put him on the top of the FBI's Most Wanted List. He was killed by law enforcement officers in Ohio in 1934.

ALL OF THESE EXAMPLES show the landscape of Arkansas during the Depression Era. The population was mostly poor farmers struggling to survive. Certain politicians could be bribed and bought off. Organized crime figures considered the State of Arkansas to be a private playground where authorities looked the other way.

So, could a man kill another man right in the State Capital building in the middle of the day and then just walk away? The answer is yes, it happened! The only question is, was it accidental, as claimed, or did something else happen that day that was covered up by an in-house investigation? Maybe ninety years after the accident, we stop emulating the politicians of the 30's that just looked the other way. It's time to look long and hard at the facts of what happened and start asking questions.

Now that we've set the political and cultural landscape of the Arkansas in the 1930's, lets take a look at some of the individuals involved in this accident and what their roles were. The odds that a man that works for the Secretary of State would kill a man that wanted to run for Secretary of State inside the Capital by accident is astronomical. When we look at all the other factors, those odds get even longer.

This is another good time to point out that nobody is accused of any crime. It's just a book to point out the folly of not investigating the accident at the time it happened. All of these questions are left unanswered by the men that handled the events of that day. If they had simple walked away and let trained Detectives handle the investigation, these questions would have been answered then. But it was decisions by Ed McDonald that have left all these questions open for us to try and understand.

CHAPTER SIX

ALBERT SANDERS

None of the people involved in Ira Gurleys death has been a bigger mystery to me than Assistant Elevator Operator Albert Sanders. Was Assistant Elevator Operator even a real job? Did anyone else ever hold this position or title? On a technicality, I suppose you could just say that Assistant Elevator Operator was a real position, but in reality, Albert Sanders was a janitor. Although the Secretary of State office told me they had no record of anyone named Albert Sanders ever being employed through their office, the Arkansas Democrat/Gazette listed expenditures and payroll for the Secretary of State office in the newspaper. Albert Sanders was listed as being on the payroll as a janitor for 1932, and in 1931 he had been employed as a yardman. On the day Ira Gurley died, The Secretary of State stated that Albert Sanders was an Assistant Elevator Operator and that the normal Elevator Operator had been given the day off. I'm sure Mr. McDonald thought that saying Assistant Elevator Operator sounded better than saying the janitor was operating the elevator. But, in fact, it was a janitor operating the elevator that day. This information would have been made public if a real law enforcement agency had investigated this accident. Of course, by now we know that didn't happen by choice. Just for the record, if you examine the payroll documents, the position of Assistant Elevator Operator cannot be found. It never existed.

Mr. Sanders stated that he did not see Ira Gurley, and that the instant the two ladies stepped off the elevator, he started the elevator upward and began sliding the cage door closed. This leaves a big question...Why? Was his intent to leave the outer door open, which would mean someone could step into the elevator shaft and fall from the third floor to the basement? The Operator would not start the elevator until those doors were closed. Without a formal investigation, we're left with all of the what if questions. What if: Mr. Sanders did not start the elevator with the door open? What if: he waited on Ira to step into the elevator and then pinned him with the cage door before starting the elevator? How would we know? Without an investigation and interrogation we're just taking his word. But what about the two witnesses? Miss Emma Hill, employed in the State Comptroller's Office, said that as she left the elevator, Mr. Gurley stepped aside to permit her to exit. So admittedly, Ira was standing right in front of the elevator door as it arrived on the third floor. Ms. Hill also said that immediately as she stepped out of the elevator, Mr. Sanders started the elevator upward without closing the doors. Again, I'm left with the question...Why? And if he was watching so intently for the ladies to step off, how could he not have seen Ira as he stepped aside? Miss Hill's version of the tragedy was corroborated by Ms. Etta Lee Jordan, who was employed in the State Health Department.

I'll ask the question, because someone should have. If these two ladies had just witnessed a man killed in broad daylight in the State Capital Building, wouldn't they say whatever they were told to say? Fear of retribution and the loss of your job during the Depression Era was real, maybe even more so than today. I would have more faith in their story if they had been separated and questioned by trained law enforcement. But no one seemed to think that was necessary. Mr. Sanders story would be more believable if he had been interrogated, but instead, he was sent home.

Another sticking point with me is the professionalism shown by Mr. Sanders after the accident. For a janitor that was just covering the elevator operator position, he certainly knew what to do if you accidentally crush someone! One would think that he would have panicked. Perhaps maybe he would have called out to the ladies that had just got off the elevator to call for help. But that didn't happen in this case. Instead, he pulled Ira into the elevator and immediately headed to the basement, where he notified Ed McDonald. And from that point on, Ed McDonald handled everything. That's awfully professional from a man we're told was running the elevator with the doors open. We were also told Mr. Sanders was so shook up, that he couldn't stay to be questioned by investigators. He killed Ira Gurley, told Ed McDonald what happened, and then left the building. They'd be hard pressed to get away with this in today's world. And you have to ask yourself, if someone had just killed someone and was so upset that they looked as if they could collapse, would you send them out to their car to drive home? I think most of us would have found a safe place for him to lie down, but nothing here was done in a way that makes sense.

I play this scene over and over in my head, and never does it make sense. Why was the elevator started with the door open? Why wouldn't have Mr. Sanders seen Ira standing in front of the door on the third floor? Why once Ira passed the ladies, trying to get onto the elevator, didn't the ladies hear or see anything else? Not the screams of Ira Gurley, not the crushing of a body, not the panic of the Janitor operating the elevator....they heard nothing.

I made a call to the Prosecuting Attorneys office in Little Rock just to inquire if any charges were ever filed against Albert Sanders. I was told they needed five days to check, but would absolutely call back the next week to let me know if charges had been filed. They never called me back and I'm guessing that means they found nothing. I tried calling back, and the message on the phone said nobody was available to speak unless you have an active case. I decided not to call again, since there was no reason to waste their time and no charges of any kind were ever mentioned in any of the newspapers.

For those wondering if Albert Sanders was just a young man playing with the elevators to see how fast he could get from one floor to the other, Albert was 50 years old. Certainly not a hot rod kid at the control of the elevator.

	1932	1931
	$1,408.33	$1,408.33
Capitol Building.		
Ed F. McDonald, custodian	$ 83.34	$ 83.33
Jim B. Higgins, assistant custodian	250.00	250.00
E. Wallin, guide	125.00	
George B. Searles, electrician		123.00
Bob Searles, fireman		100.00
Albert Sanders, yardman		100.00
Fred Albright, janitor		60.00
Letha Johnson, janitor		60.00
Paul Lysell, janitor		60.00
Hugh White, janitor		60.00
S. H. Sacker, electrician	125.00	
W. L. Halbert, night watchman	125.00	125.00
John Morton, fireman	100.00	
Charlie Holt, yardman	100.00	
L. O. Moore, gardener	100.00	
G. G. Dandridge, chief janitor	125.00	125.00
Steve Russell, janitor	60.00	60.00
Eli Cooper, janitor	60.00	
Jim Thompson, janitor	60.00	60.00
Columbus Toomer, janitor	60.00	60.00
Frank Crawford, janitor	60.00	60.00
Patria Wines, janitor	60.00	60.00
Rosie Humphrey, janitor	60.00	60.00
Jack Johnson, janitor	60.00	60.00
Marnette Callaway, janitor	60.00	60.00
Reece Fitzgerald, janitor	60.00	60.00
Jake McCollum, janitor	60.00	60.00
Albert Sanders, janitor	60.00	
Lonetta Buckley, janitor	60.00	
V. P. Mitchell, janitor	60.00	
P. G. Smith, capital policeman	100.00	100.00
Raphael Raynor, elevator operator	100.00	100.00
	$2,173.34	$1,948.33

State Department Pay Rolls

Continuing the publication of state-house pay rolls, the Gazette today lists the employes and salaries of the offices of the secretary of state and the comptroller for February of 1931 and of 1932.

SECRETARY OF STATE.

	1932	1931
Ed F. McDonald, secretary of state	$ 333.33	$ 333.33
P. A. Rowland, deputy	225.00	225.00
Horace B. Higgins, deputy	225.00	225.00
Miss Emma C. Riley, clerk	175.00	175.00
Geo. W. Neal, clerk	175.00	175.00
Mrs. M. D. McClain, clerk	150.00	150.00
Mrs. V. C. McDonald, clerk-stenographer	125.00	125.00
	$1,408.33	$1,408.33

Capitol Building.

	1932	1931
Ed F. McDonald, custodian	$ 83.34	$ 83.33
Jim B. Higgins, assistant custodian	250.00	250.00
R. Wallin, guide	125.00	
George B. Searles, electrician		125.00
Bob Searles, fireman		100.00
Albert Sanders, yardman		100.00
Fred Albright, janitor		65.00
Letha Johnson, janitor		60.00
Paul Lynch, janitor		65.00
Hugh White, janitor		65.00
S. H. Sacker, electrician	125.00	
W. L. Halbert, night watchman	125.00	125.00
John Morten, fireman	100.00	
Charlie Holt, yardman	100.00	
L. O. Moore, gardener	100.00	
G. G. Dandridge, chief janitor	175.00	175.00
Steve Russell, janitor	60.00	60.00
Eli Cooper, janitor	60.00	
Jim Thompson, janitor	60.00	60.00
Columbus Toomer, janitor	60.00	60.00
Frank Crawford, janitor	60.00	60.00
Patria Wines, janitor	60.00	60.00
Rosie Humphrey, janitor	60.00	60.00
Jack Johnson, janitor	60.00	60.00
Marnette Callaway, janitor	60.00	60.00
Reece Fitzgerald, janitor	60.00	60.00
Jake McCollum, janitor	60.00	60.00
Albert Sanders, janitor	60.00	
Loretta Buckley, janitor	60.00	
V. P. Mitchell, janitor	60.00	
F. G. Smith, capital policeman	100.00	100.00
Raphael Raynor, elevator operator	100.00	100.00
	$3,133.34	$1,948.32
Grand total, Secretary of state's Department	$3,381.67	$3,356.66

AUDITORIAL DEPARTMENT.

	1932	1931
Howard Reed, comptroller	$ 414.66	$ 414.66
T. B. Kitchens, assistant comptroller (deceased)		250.00
D. H. Balsour, auditor	225.00	225.00
Charles M. Clergel, auditor	225.00	225.00
Julian Hogan, examiner	300.00	300.00
Marie Trimble, clerk	150.00	150.00

"The list of county accountants below was obtained from the February pay roll filed by the comptroller's office in the state auditor's office."

J. Bryan Sims, chief county accountant	$ 325.00
Ora Lee Smith, clerk	150.00
Luther Drake, auditor	200.00
W. H. Phipps, auditor	200.00
Jeda Johnson, auditor	200.00
Marion Douglas, auditor	200.00
W. R. Hardy, auditor	200.00
Vint Addy, auditor	200.00
J. Gayle Windsor, auditor	200.00
Alton Durden, auditor	200.00
Frank Storey, auditor	200.00
Kirby Smith, auditor	200.00
James M. Deal, auditor	200.00
Bruce Fraser, auditor	200.00
H. D. Campbell, extra auditor	200.00
B. Massingill, auditor	200.00
Wirt Boud, auditor	200.00
F. V. McCoy, assistant chief accountant	200.00
	$4,531.66

Appended are explanations by Mr. Reed: "Mr. Kitchen's position was replaced by a $200 per month employe.

County audit division changed in part April 1, 1931, from counties to state, 34 counties being added and the salary of the chief county accountant being raised from $300 to $325 a month, and the clerk's salary being raised to $150. The county field accountants' force was paid $10 per day each by the counties, but each of the present staff of 15 auditors is paid $200 per month. The law allows assistant chief county accountant $250 a month, but he is being paid $200. Department employe's warrants are being discounted 10 per cent, which several other departments, by reason of being collecting agencies, are not required to do.

CHAPTER SEVEN
ED F. McDONALD
ARKANSAS SECRETARY OF STATE
1931-1937

As a public servant, I'm sure there is a long list of good things done, and wonderful accomplishments performed by Ed McDonald. Ninety years after the fact, I cannot tell you the heart of the man, nor the motives for how he handled the accident of 1932. All we can do is list the facts of what occurred and decide for ourselves if everything was handled appropriately. It wasn't, and this book has tried to stress how many ways the accident was dealt with in a less than professional manner. After reading all of the facts that we are allowed to know, nothing in the case seems on the up and up. One is left thinking that either Mr. McDonald was not very bright and handled everything wrong...or...we're left to think that Mr. McDonald was a very conniving individual that sought to control and mislead the public.

The number one question that keeps coming back to me is why didn't Mr. McDonald simply say that due to the seriousness of the accident, and due to wanting to avoid the appearance of impropriety, I'm turning this investigation over to local law enforcement. But, counter to that, it seems Mr. McDonald was adamant about handling this investigation himself. Sure, he called in the Coroner, but that was another Democrat elected official, and the Coroner was needed to officially declare the death an accident. A co-member of the Arkansas Game and Fish Commission, Guy

Amsler, was allowed to join in the investigation. This makes little sense until you discover that Guy Amsler was an attorney that represented the State. So Guy Amsler was not there for the benefit of Ira Gurley, he was there for the benefit of Ed McDonald. So just like we're told that Albert Sanders is the Assistant Elevator Operator and not the Janitor, we're told that guy Amsler is a co-worker of Ira Gurley and not that he is a lawyer. So now, with this information, we understand a little clearer why Guy Amsler was there, and it wasn't because he sat on a Commission with Ira Gurley.

There's only one story of the events that day in 1932, and that's Ed McDonald's story. And it seems nobody questioned that story, and perhaps, that makes a statement of the conditions and time of the era. Ed McDonald sent the main witness, Albert Sanders, home, which means from that point on, any telling of the events is second hand. The "official" investigation is supposedly the Coroners investigation, and he never spoke to Albert Sanders! He ruled the death officially an accident by listening to a second hand story from someone that wasn't even there.

There was a reason Ed McDonald wanted to handle the investigation. There was a reason he sent Albert Sanders home. And there's got to be a reason Ed McDonald did not want any Police agency involved. The problem is, we'll never know those reasons.

Since Ira Gurley had announced his intentions to run for Secretary of State, which was Ed McDonald's office, it seems absurd that McDonald would be in charge of this investigation, but he was. And after the death, he followed the body back to Green Forest, Arkansas to attend the funeral. He even was named as one of the Honorary Pallbearers at Ira Gurley's funeral. That's either one compassionate man, or one cruel human being, but you'll have to decide for yourselves.

I've included a case from 1934 that tells of a lawsuit filed by the Bank Commissioner against Ed McDonald. To me, it said much of Mr. McDonald's allegiance.

McDONALD VS. WASSON

(1934)

The Arkansas Supreme Court heard arguments in a lawsuit filed by Marion Wasson, Bank Commissioner, against Ed McDonald, Secretary of State. When broken down to layman terms, the suit claims that as the State of Arkansas' Bank Commissioner, all banks in Arkansas fall under his jurisdiction and regulations as set forth by the State Legislature. Ed McDonald contended that separate Banking Co-ops filed for banking between a group of investors was different from a normal bank and therefore should not fall under the jurisdiction of the Bank commissioner. So who would they file paperwork with to conduct business? The answer would be the Secretary of State office completely unattached and unsupervised by the Banking Commission.

The meaning of this is that certain groups of individuals didn't have to put their money in the same bank that you and I would have used. Which in 1934, during the Great Depression, it was fact that many banks were going bankrupt and shutting down. There banking co-ops would be private banks, and the source of income and the source of outcome were not under the supervision of the Banking Commission.

We know that a large majority of the average Arkansas population had very little to no money during this period. I have also written about who did have money, and lots of it, during this time in Arkansas. The average corner bank where normal citizens kept their savings would not have done for these men, but a private banking co-op outside of the Banking Commission rules, would have been very attractive to them. This made Secretary of State Ed McDonald a very important man to the co-ops.

Marion Wasson had a strong argument and stated that under law, he had: Duly made and promulgated, and the requisite number of members of the Bank Advisory Council of the said State duly approved, rules and regulations relating to the organization, supervision, control, liquidation and dissolution of the cooperative banking associations aforesaid, which said rules and regulations were so made and promulgated, and were so approved, under pursuant to the provisions of act 88 of the Acts of the General Assembly of said State for the year 1933. A copy of the said rules and regulations bearing the signature and seal of office of the said plaintiff, and the signatures of said members of said Bank Advisory Council, and marked Exhibit A, is hereto attached as a part of this complaint.

The Bank Commission did not want there bank co-ops filing articles of incorporation with the Secretary of States office, but through the Bank Commission, as all other banks did. That would not be agreeable to some money investors, and borrowing from the old saying, "where there's a will, there's a way", lets just say, "where there's a will, there's a loophole."

The Supreme Court opinion was that since the act 88 had no repealing clause found in it anywhere, a implied repeal could not be expressed. Which means that prior laws allowing the co-op banks could still stand as a separate bank from the banks under the supervision of the Bank Commission.

Ask yourself, "who wins here?" The farmer in the fields?...No. The factory workers?...No. Teachers?...No. In the 1930's there was a very small group of men that had money, and most of them were not from the State of Arkansas. There men could bank in a co-op bank that the normal citizen was not allowed to use. And they did not have to answer to the State Banking Commission.

I include this lawsuit as a testament to where the concerns and loyalties of the Secretary of State were at during this time. People were starving, and when I say people, I mean your grandparents and relatives that suffered through the Depression in Arkansas. Knowing the miserable conditions of poor common citizens trying to manage day to day to feed their families, it speaks loudly to me to see what our elected officials were up to while the common man struggled. So not only did Ed McDonald not have to operate within the normal laws that you and I would have to obey when Ira Gurley died, but it appears he was working to see to it that special interest groups did not have to fall under Bank Commission guidelines.

Arkansas began the decade of the 1930's with 420 banks, and concluded it with 234. The head of the largest bank, American Exchange Trust, was convicted of accepting deposits in a bank he knew to be insolvent. He was sentenced to a year in prison, but he received a gubernatorial pardon.

In a twist, while lawsuits were being contested here in Arkansas to get bank co-ops out from under the scrutiny of the Bank Commission, on the Federal level, the Federal Deposit Insurance Corporation or FDIC was created in 1933 to insure bank deposits and to subject state chartered banks to further government oversight.

With this ruling: A group of investors could file paperwork with the Secretary of State office to operate a co-op bank. If approved, they did not have to file any paperwork with the State

Banking Commission, nor did they have to abide by the rules and regulations of the Banking Commission. And it was all legal. With the in-flow and out-flow of money not regulated, you do not have to be a lawyer to see where the opportunity for illegal activity to take place.

CHAPTER EIGHT

ELECTIONS OF 1932

Let's look at the election results of 1932 and the office seekers. The entire country had been hit hard by the stock market crash of 1929, which had left the nation in the pits of a deep Depression, both economically and mentally. There were cries for change, but one advantage the Democrat's of the day had, was the perception that this Depression was caused by a Republican Administration, and particularly President Herbert Hoover. Of course, in Arkansas, all of the elected officials to State wide office were Democrats, so the Democrat Primary would hold the key to who got elected.

In the Presidential Elections of 1932, Franklin D. Roosevelt defeated Herbert Hoover by an 85.9% to 12.9% margin in Arkansas. His "New Deal" policy was very popular in the State, which was struggling with high unemployment and poor prospects for agriculture, which represented most of the Arkansas economy.

In the Arkansas Governor's race, Junius Marion Futrell defeated James Livesay by carrying all 75 counties in the State. Futrell had 90.4% of the votes, compared to Livesay having 8.9%. Futrell, a Chancery Judge, had won a seven candidate primary over six other Democrats seeking the office.

In the Arkansas Lt. Governor's race, the incumbent, Lawrence Wilson, faced a six man primary battle for re-election. Even though Democrat voters had historically given two two-year terms to their elected candidates, Wilson had become embroiled in scandals after pardoning his brother from a ten year prison sentence while serving as acting Governor, and in his capacity to dissolve three insolvent banks in his home county. Candidates in the Primary were Lt. Governor Wilson, Lee Cazort, Paul Grabiel, Fred Hutto, Joe Kimysey, R. F. Milwee, and J. Rossner Venable. The election was won by Lee Cazort.

In the Arkansas Attorney General race, Hal L. Norwood won re-election. The race was a little confusing for voters since one of the other candidates in the race was named Hal C. Norwood. Three other candidates in the race were Boyd Cypert, John Sheffield, and J. G. Ragsdale.

In the Arkansas State Auditor race, J. Oscar Humphrey won re-election. He was challenged in the Democrat Primary by Roy H. Hand and Charlie Parker.

In the Arkansas State Land Commissioner race, the incumbent, Belva Martin, did not pursue re-election. Three men sought the Democrat nomination. They were William DeCamp, George Neal, and Ed Rosser. The election was won by George Neal.

In the Arkansas Secretary of State race, Ed. F. McDonald won re-election. He was unopposed.

Let that sink in for just a minute. You've just read a list of over two dozen candidates that were seeking statewide office. All of the offices listed were hotly contested races with multiple candidates vying for election. Yet, Ed McDonald was unopposed. There may have been many reason's given for nobody wanting to run for Secretary of State, and we'll never know for sure why Mr. McDonald had no opposition. But I'm going to state the obvious here...could it possibly be because a man that stated he wanted to run for Secretary of State was crushed to death in the Capital building by one of the States employees and nobody else dared run? We have no way to know for sure, and we're left with speculation as what possible candidates may or may not have been thinking. But I know what I would have been thinking, if I was around in 1932.

CHAPTER NINE
THE GURLEY FAMILY
AFTER THE ACCIDENT

Ira had moved his family to Little Rock while he was serving in the Arkansas House of Representatives. His wife, Cleo, moved the girls back to Carroll County after his death. Cleo then decided that the best thing for her daughters was to leave the State of Arkansas and move to Los Angeles, California. Cleo had family there and felt the change would be good for her and the girls. Cleo was very close with her family in Carroll County, so this move must have been a big sacrifice for her. This trait of being close to family was passed down to Mary and Helen, and they kept close with their mother all through her life.

Losing a husband and father would be enough tragedy for any family, but more heartache awaited the family when they arrived in California. In a cruel twist of fate, it was only a few months after the move that the oldest daughter, Mary, contacted polio. This family was surviving the Great Depression and the death of Ira, and now Mary had a devastating crippling and life-threatening disease that was prevalent during the era. Cleo, Mary, and Helen must have thought that they had to fight some kind of curse each day. It's a stroke of luck that these three girls had each other. They developed a bond that lasted a life time, and were always close. They needed this bond now that Mary was paralyzed. It's estimated that during the 1940's outbreak of polio, it disabled an average of more than 35,000 people each year. Even the President of the United States, Franklin Delano Roosevelt was thought to be disabled by polio.

The youngest daughter, Helen, avoided the disease and attended High School at John H. Francis Polytechnic High School.

After Helen graduated from high school, the family moved to Warm Springs, Georgia for Mary to be treated for her polio. During this time, Helen left to attend one semester at Texas State College for Women, and then moved back to California to attend Woodbury Business College. Helen graduated from Woodbury in 1941. In 1947, Cleo and Mary moved back to Cleo's native home of Osage, Arkansas in Carroll County, while Helen stayed in Los Angeles. The polio that Mary had contracted in her early 20's resulted in her spending the rest of her life paralyzed from the waist down. She did marry, and became Mary Gurley Alford. It was reported that Helen aided Mary in her later years while Mary battled her conditions. Cleo also married and became Cleo Sisco Bryan. Cleo passed away in 1980 and Mary passed away in 1987.

I'll write more about Helen Gurley and all of her accomplishments in another chapter. Considering her background and family tragedies, she was able to turn her life into a monumental success. No doubt showing some of the savvy and drive passed down to her by her father.

If you visit the tiny community of Osage, Arkansas today, you'll find Cleo, Mary, Helen, along with their husbands, all buried there in the Sisco Family cemetery. Still together into eternity, showing the unity the ladies developed in their struggle to survive after Ira's death. After surviving all the tragedies this family suffered through, that included the death of Ira, the Great Depression, and fighting polio, one can only guess that after all this hardship, there was nobody they'd rather face eternity with.

When reading about these ladies, one has to be impressed with their drive and fortitude as they faced lifes problems. Cleo had to be a strong lady with great determination to raise her daughters. All three of these ladies left a lasting impression.

CHAPTER TEN
HELEN GURLEY BROWN

Ira and Cleo Gurley youngest daughter, Helen, would have turned 100 in 2022 if she were still alive. She passed away on August 13, 2012 in New York City. As a writer and historian, it is with great sadness that I say I never had the pleasure to meet Helen. She was a 10 year old child when her father died, and I would have loved to ask her what memories she had of Ira. From the time of his death in 1932 and her passing in 2012 those memories must have become faint, but still, I would have loved to hear her speak of him.

I also think about if Ira had lived a long life, there's a good chance I would have met the man. Especially, if he had returned to Carroll County in his retirement. An interview with him would have been very interesting, and I'm sorry we were all deprived of hearing him reflect. I also wonder what his opinions of his daughters work would have been. She was controversial for her day, talking about subjects most women only blushed about. But that's what put her on the cutting edge and separated her from so many other writers. I think Ira would have told us she got some of the grit and determination from him, but we'll never know for sure. An interview with Ira and Helen both would have been a writers dream come true.

Helen had began a career that was destined for success shortly after graduating from business college. After working at the William Morris Agency, Music Corporation of America, and Jaffe talent agency, Helen worked for Foote Cone and Belding advertising agency as a secretary. Her employer recognized something special in her writing skills and moved her to the copywriting department, where she advanced rapidly to become one of the nation's highest paid ad copywriters in the early 1960's. She was a woman competing in a man's world and winning. A woman working as a copywriter in the early 1960's was very rare. All of her coworkers may not have accepted her in the office, but they all had to accept the fact that she was out performing them. Some thought that the only place for a woman in the business world was as a secretary, but Helen had her sights sets much higher, and she had the abilities to attain her goals.

In 1959 Helen married David Brown, who would go on to become a highly successful film Producer in Hollywood. Some of the films he would Produce were blockbusters like The Sting, Jaws, Cocoon, Driving Miss Daisy, and the list keeps going with many more. Any other Producer in Hollywood would be hard pressed to match his resume.

In 1962, her book Sex And The Single Girl was published in 28 Countries, and stayed on the Best Seller list for over a year. The book was made into a movie in 1964 starring Natalie Wood. In 1965, Helen became Editor-In-Chief of Cosmopolitan Magazine. At the time, it was noted for "high brow" content, but Helen reinvented it as a magazine for the modern single career woman. The sales increased and both Helen and Cosmopolitan became successful style and trendsetters. Helen was Editor-In-Chief for 32 years and even after stepping down from that position, she still served as Editor for the magazines foreign editions. She had guided Cosmopolitan Magazine with great skill and built a fashion and style empire.

And yet, despite all of the success and wealth she attained, on the occasion of her death Helen wished to be brought back home to Carroll County, Arkansas. She is laid to rest between her husband, David, and her beloved mother, Cleo. Her tombstone isn't fancy, or made to look like a memorial, but looks similar to everyone else's in the cemetery. It's simple and plain. It has the appearance of a girl that wanted to come home and return to her roots with her family, and leave all the glamour behind. She and her husband had acquired enough wealth to be buried anywhere in the world, but she wanted to lie next to her mother. This states loudly about the bond the girls had formed.

I want to write a few words in defense of Helen Gurley Brown and her lack of activity in her home town of Green Forest, Arkansas. Without looking at all of the facts, one might think that she "simply got too big to care," or was embarrassed of her birth place. But a number of reasons could explain her reluctance to return back to her roots while she was still living. First and foremost, she was a ten year old little girl when her father was crushed in an elevator in Arkansas. Knowing what we have learned in the contents of this book, perhaps she and family didn't want anything to do with Arkansas after her fathers death. I never spoke to Helen about her feelings toward her fathers death, so I can only imagine the fear and confusion this caused her. I think any of us that had a tragedy like this happen in our family, if we left the State, would we want to come back? And let's look at the second reason she returned so seldom to Arkansas. Did she feel welcomed? Was she welcomed? Helen wrote a very controversial book in 1962, Sex And The Single Girl, which would have certainly raised eyebrows in 1960's Carroll County, Arkansas. The book was shocking for it's day, as Helen wrote about single professional women living the single life, in a day when the "norm" was for women to find a good man and save herself for marriage. Helen may not have been the only one that saw the future that was coming, but she was bold enough to write about it. This may have not put Helen on the top of the list for invitations back in Arkansas. So, maybe she thought Arkansas didn't want her to come back! And if one needed a third reason, you can also see that once she became Editor-In-Chief of Cosmopolitan Magazine, her time was filled with stories, promotions, deadlines, and appointments that kept her busy in New York. Finding time for events in Arkansas would have been hard to find for such a busy lady.

I remember as a very young man, watching Helen Gurley Brown during an appearance on The Tonight Show with Johnny Carson. Johnny mentioned to Helen that he had grown up in Nebraska and knew that she had come from a small town in Arkansas. Helen immediately became uncomfortable, and she had a look of disdain on her face that almost looked pained. She reluctantly acknowledged that, yes, she was from Green Forest,

Arkansas as she shifted in her seat and tugged on her dress. I remember thinking how disappointed I was that she was not proud to have come from Arkansas and attained her current position. I was disappointed, but looking back now, I feel sorry for Helen. So much was stolen from her and we can't comprehend what she went through to get where she was. I have even more respect for her today. Helen Gurley Brown will go down in history as one of the most successful businesswomen in the history of Arkansas.

CHAPTER ELEVEN
RECONSTRUCTING THE DAY

I think the best way to develop an opinion of something that happened ninety years ago, is to take the facts of what we know and lay them out one by one in order. We know this happened in June, which in Arkansas is always hot and humid. Most days in Summer the humidity is so bad that you sweat just standing in the shade. Tempers flare easily in weather like this, and that's just a fact. It was the lunch hour, which is always a hectic time. People have a set amount of time to grab a bite to eat and are always in a hurry. The Arkansas State Capital can be a very busy and hectic location with hundreds of people working, lobbying, and sightseeing. With a Great Depression choking the job market, the Capital was one place that stayed busy through it all. Legislatures still had to legislate and make laws, even in troubled times.

We know that Ira Gurley had served in the Arkansas House of Representatives in four consecutive terms. He then had accepted a position on the Arkansas Game and Fish Commission. We also know that Ira Gurley had let his intentions be known that he was going to run for the office of Secretary of State. This fact alone tells me that Ira Gurley and Ed McDonald were not exactly political allies, since Ira wanted to unseat Ed from his office. But I have no evidence at all that says Ira and Ed were in personal conflict. Common sense for most of us says that if you were going to run for office, you wouldn't necessarily pick the office of someone you liked and respected to run against. Obviously, Ira saw a problem in the Secretary of State office, and thought he would be better choice for the voters of Arkansas than the man currently holding the office. I think it's fairly safe to say that as a general rule, you do not run for office against your good friend, or even someone that you would choose to be a pallbearer at your funeral.

So, on the day of the accident, Ira Gurley, a man that had stated his intentions to run for Secretary of State, was hurrying to catch an elevator on the third floor of the Capital Building. The normal elevator operator had been given the day off and the man that Ed McDonald described as the Assistant Elevator Operator was in charge of the elevator. But, we've already discovered that Assistant Elevator Operator is not a real position that shows up on the payrolls at the Capital building. The man operating the elevator is Albert Sanders, which payroll records tell us worked at the Capital as a Janitor. Before becoming a Janitor, Albert had been employed at the Capital as a Yardman. Once again, I think it's fairly safe to say that Albert Sanders did not have a lot of experience operating an elevator. His conduct on this day would attest to that fact.

As the elevator arrived on the third floor, it was occupied by two ladies that worked in the Capital, Miss Emma Hill, employed in the State Comptrollers Office, and Miss Etta Lee Jordan, who was employed in the State Health Department. In all likelihood, both of these ladies were on the elevator by coincidence and just happened to be at a horrible place at a horrible time when the accident occurred. Still, it would have been nice if professional law enforcement officers had been given the chance to separate the two ladies and interrogate them. I think if I had just stepped off of an elevator and a man was crushed to death, I'd have more to say than, "What he said is true, I noticed the elevator starting immediately as I stepped off, and Mr. Gurley rushed by me, and that's all I saw."

Both ladies said the exact same thing, and that seems a little odd to me, as if it had been rehearsed.

When the elevator reached the third floor, the elevator would have stopped and the main door would have opened. Mr. Sanders would then slide the cage door across to open it so the ladies could exit. It was stated by the witnesses that Ira Gurley was standing right in front of the door as it opened. How Albert Sanders failed to see him would be a mystery, since Ira had to step sideways to allow the ladies to exit. There's a very good chance that Albert would have known who Ira was. Albert worked at the Capital as one of the Janitors, and before that he worked there as a Yardman. Ira had served eight years in the House of Representatives and would have been a familiar face. We're told, Albert didn't speak to Ira or acknowledge him. It's likely that Albert knew exactly who Ira was, and that Ira was planning on running for Secretary of State. Discussions of that nature would have been common among employees wondering if a new Secretary of State might want to replace some of the old Secretary of States people. And this would have been extremely important during this period in history when jobs were just not available to be found. If a man had a job, he'd want to keep it at all cost.

As Ira stepped aside, the two ladies exited the elevator. At this point, Albert Sanders supposedly told Ed McDonald that he started the elevator up without closing the doors. Nobody thought to ask why, which is a great question to ask, because why would you take an elevator up while leaving the doors open, when people would be at risk of walking into the open elevator shaft and falling to the basement floor four floors down? But despite the absurdity of this claim, he supposedly started the elevator up and accidentally pinned Ira in the door frame. To slide a door closed and pin someone in the door frame, you have to be closing that door with some force, some very heavy force. Ira would have been pushing back and yelling, but the door was being held tight enough to keep him in place. The fact that Ira was pinned in the doorway while being crushed is pivotal to the part of the story saying the elevator was already in motion when Ira tried to jump on. Otherwise, the door would have hit Ira, and Albert would have apologized, and that would have been the end of the story. But when you put the elevator in motion first, and then slide the door, it explains the accidental death. So even though it makes no sense what so ever that Albert was starting the elevator with the doors open, it had to be part of the story. Without the elevator in motion part of the story, you'd just have a murder. So I understand why Albert and Ed stressed this part of the story, even if there was no explanation why, or reason for doing it.

As the body of Ira stood trapped and crushed in the doorway, Albert calmly stopped the elevator, opened the cage door, pulled Ira inside, and took the elevator to the basement. This is a real sticking point for me. Two ladies had just stepped off the elevator and couldn't have been more than five or six steps away from the elevator. Ira must have screamed in first terror, and second agony. Albert should have been shocked and horrified, and complete pandemonium should have broken out on the third floor when this happened. But it did not. Albert pulled the body inside the elevator and took it to the basement, where he notified Ed McDonald. We were told that an ambulance was called for Ira, and that it arrived within minutes. We'll have to take their word on this fact too, since no reports were made. On one hand, Albert Sanders is an unprofessional clown running the elevators with the doors open, and then in a snap, he's calm enough not to panic when he crushed a man to death. His actions were very professional indeed, as if a Janitor operating the elevator had practiced what to do in the case of an accidental crushing of a passenger. There's not a Detective alive that wouldn't want to interrogate Albert Sanders. Too bad it never happened, because Ed McDonald decided he'd handle the investigation himself. The Arkansas State Capital is outside the jurisdiction of the local Police Department and have the authority to handle accidents in-house. But the appearance of an impropriety would have led most elected officials to step aside and ask another agency to come in and investigate. The Little Rock Police Department and the Pulaski County Sheriff's Office were available, but Ed McDonald didn't want the investigating. He would do it himself.

With Ira being transported away in an ambulance, Ed McDonald decides he will handle the full investigation. First things first, the man operating the elevator, Albert Sanders, was sent home. Another absurdity in this case. Ed said that Albert was so shook up over crushing Ira that he was afraid Albert might collapse, so he sends him out to his car to drive home! Just one more piece of this puzzle that makes no sense. So now we've ha Mr. Sanders go from wild man operating elevators with the door open, to professional operator handling an emergency, to poor old Albert, he's about to collapse. It appears that the only one Ed McDonald wanted telling this story was Ed himself, even though he wasn't there in the elevator when it happened. Again, every Detective is thinking how great it would have been to have Albert interrogated. Sometimes people remember details that they may have overlooked and sometimes details change when being retold. But that interrogation never happened.

Next, Ed interviewed the two ladies to collaborate Albert's story. We have to take his word on that, because all through this, we're reminded that no report was made. Did he interview them? Is it possible he told them what to say? Ninety years later, all we can do is wonder and wish things had been handled differently. But if all of this is on the up and up, then we're led to believe that the two ladies collaborated each others story exactly the same.

By now, word had reached the Capital that Ira Gurley was pronounced dead in the ambulance before ever making it to the hospital. So now Ed McDonald needed someone else involved in the investigation, he needed the Coroner. The Coroner was another elected official named Dr. Samuel Boyce. The doctor was invited to come to the Capital and conduct an investigation. And another man was invited to join in on the investigation as well, Guy Amsler, that sat on the Arkansas Game and Fish Commission. Another point that made no sense at all until you discover that Mr. Amsler was an attorney and Ed McDonald wanted his lawyer with him during this investigation. We now have Secretary of State, Ed McDonald, an attorney, Guy Amsler, and the Coroner, Dr. Samuel Boyce doing the investigation of Ira's death. These three men are going to determine if this death was accidental and the man that was operating the elevator, Albert Sanders, has already been sent home. It looks like Albert didn't need to be there since Ed McDonald was going to do all of the talking for him. But who was there to give a voice for Ira Gurley? The answer is nobody.

Dr. Boyce and Guy Amsler listened to Ed McDonald tell his story of the accident. They are said to have talked to the two ladies from the elevator that dutifully relay their story again. Eureka! Dr. Boyce is ready to pronounce the cause of death...ACCIDENT. Just like that...ACCIDENT...case closed, no more investigation.

By listening to a second-hand story from Ed McDonald and listening to the two ladies, Dr. Boyce has declared he's heard all he needs. He officially declares the death of Ira Gurley an accident. Case closed.

Ira Gurley deserved better.

CHAPTER TWELVE
THE FUNERAL OF IRA GURLEY

I ra Gurley's body was returned home to Green Forest, Arkansas. He was returning home to be buried as a local and State role model and leader to all that had come to know, or know of, him. A large part of Carroll County showed up for the funeral with State and local dignitaries in attendance. The funeral was held on a Sunday afternoon, so most of Carroll County would have attended Church service before making their way to the funeral. Everything about the incident had moved very quickly, as evidenced by the fact that Ira died during the noon hour on Friday, his body was returned to Green Forest at 10:30 in the evening on Saturday, and he was buried at 2:00 on Sunday afternoon. A mere 50 hours from death to burial. It would have taken much longer if suspension of foul play or possible negligent homicide charges had been filed. We'll always be left to wonder what may have been found if Ira had undergone an autopsy. But this crack team of investigators saw no need for anything except a funeral.

Take a deep breath and make sure you're sitting down. I'm going to list the pallbearers at the funeral, and there's a couple of names that may raise an eyebrow.

Pallbearers at Ira's funeral were J. E. Gregson, Luther Owens, J. W. Trimble, and Ted Coxsey of Berryville. Ray Anderson and Massey Seitz of Green Forest. W. A. Rooksbery and Guy Amsler of Little Rock.

The list of Honorary Pallbearers is long and full of representatives from around the State of Arkansas. The Honorary

Pallbearers were Henry Wilson and B. O. George of Berryville. Harry Neely of Searcy. Judge G. B. Ewing of McGhee. Charles Tompkins of Prescott. W. N. Deaton of Conway. C. M. sisco of Siloam Springs. W. R. Phillips, Elmer Reeves, C. C. O'Neal, W. J. Tate, and John Stafford, all of Green Forest. Albert Bell, Frank Whittaker, and L. C. Brown, all of Alpena Pass. F. O. Butts and C. A. Fuller of Eureka Springs. A. J. Russell, Ed McDonald, Lee Miles, Jim B. Higgins, P. A. Rowland, E. I. McKinley, Floyd Sharp, Ed R. Hicks, Jimmy Newcomb, W. A. Mann, H. O. Topf, Roy V. Leonard, Ira C. Susky, R. C. Gibson, Dr. G. M. Reagan, A. R. Lamb, and Judge Turner Butler, all of Little Rock.

I don't know if anyone other than me is more than a little surprised seeing the names Ed McDonald and Guy Amsler on the list of Pallbearers, but considering the circumstances of Ira's death, I was actually disgusted when I read their names on the list. For One: Ira was going to run for Ed's office. For Two: It was one of Ed's employees that killed Ira. And for Three: Ed had done everything in his power to keep official law enforcement out of the investigation. So now, Ed has run the investigation, followed the body to Green Forest, and is an Honorary Pallbearer at the funeral service.

The man certainly saw this through to the end. It seems every aspect of this incident was under the control of Ed McDonald, from the time of the accident, to the burial.

There are many names on the list of Pallbearers that are very honorable men. Men that I have researched, read, and studied about, and have been left with a feeling of respect for their accomplishments and sacrifices. The only names I question on the list are Ed McDonald and Guy Amsler, who seem to be everywhere in this story. My reasons are that Mr. McDonald left to many open questions in his investigation for me to have a clear picture of exactly what happened. I wish he would have stepped aside, just to be open, honest, and above reproach in this incident. But he'd have none of that, and that was his choice.

CHAPTER THIRTEEN
JUST ME THINKING OUT LOUD

By now, maybe you have formed some idea of what you think really happened on that day in June of 1932. You don't know for sure, nobody can know for sure, but you and I have some idea that something about this accident just does not sound as being on the level. Was this a complete accidental death? Was this a murder and cover-up? Is it something in between? There are so many questions not answered in this story, that it leaves one frustrated by the lack of, or the demand for, more answers when this event took place. I'm going to give a few scenarios of what might have happened that day. They're just logical guesses of what might have happened, and I have no proof of wrong doing. Other than the disaster of an investigation into this accident.

Scenario #1... everything they said is true. The assistant elevator operator was operating the elevator with the door open. Ira tried to jump onto a moving elevator, got caught in the door frame, and was crushed to death. Terrible accident, and the only one to blame was Ira for trying to leap onto a moving elevator...end of story.

Even if you accept this story, (which I find hard to believe), how is negligent homicide charges not brought against Albert Sanders? If any of you reading this and go out and operate an elevator with the door open, and someone dies as a result, you will be charged. Why wasn't Mr. Sanders?

Scenario #2... It was all planned. Ira was called to the Capital building for a meeting. The elevator operator was given the day off so that someone in on the plan can be placed at the controls.

That someone is one of the Janitors they refer to as the Assistant Elevator Operator. They knew Ira had intentions of running for Secretary of State and that he would be a strong candidate. Ira was intentionally pinned in the doorway of the elevator and crushed in the door frame. Albert was told what to do as soon as he had completed this task. He took the body to the basement and Ed McDonald met him there to take over from that point. Albert Sanders was sent home and Ed McDonald handled all aspects of the investigation, including telling the story of the accident and seeing to it that the witnesses knew what to say when the Coroner arrived.

Even if this has any truth to it at all, it can't be proven. And if you can't prove it, you can't positively say that without a doubt that this happened. It would have taken a confession from someone involved, and we do not have that. We're left asking ourselves if the reason we do not have a confession is because no real investigation was ever done. What would Albert Sanders story have been under interrogation? Or what would the two ladies have said if they had been separated and interrogated? The appearance of something being covered up here is striking. If only there had been an outside agency there to do the investigation. What if there had been a trial held? If everyone was cleared of all wrong doing in a court of law, we'd have to accept those findings. But this was Arkansas in 1932 and no cries for investigations, charges, trials, or justice for Ira was heard.

Scenario #3... Is it possible that Albert Sanders went "rogue"? The normal Elevator Operator has the day off and Albert Sanders is told to take his place for the day. Albert recognized Ira Gurley and knew he had intentions to run for his bosses job. In a moment of rage, he pinned Ira in the doorway of the elevator and runs the elevator up, crushing Ira in the door frame. He takes Ira to the basement and notifies Ed McDonald. At this point we have to guess if (a)...Ed listens to Alberts story of how the accident happened and believes every word of it. Then out of compassion for the man, he sends him home to recuperate from the trauma. Or (b)...Ed realizes that one of his employees has killed a man in the Capital building and fearing retribution in the voting booths during the election, he decides to send Albert home and concocts the story of an innocent accident. In this scenario, Albert and the two ladies that were on the elevator simply repeat what they are told to say.

How would our minds dream up something so horrific? Because the entire investigation was conducted in the form of a cover up, and we're left asking, what were they covering up? It's only a scenario of how things could have happened, but we'll never know for sure.

Those are three scenarios of what might have happened. I'm not accusing anyone of doing anything other than conducting an investigation so obviously flawed, that we're left asking why?, why?, why?. That's the only thing I have proof of really, a shady investigation. But I refuse to believe that Ed McDonald was stupid or naive and had no idea that not allowing law enforcement to come in would look inappropriate. He had to know, but for some reason he couldn't let them in. It was important to him that no outside agency entered this investigation. He wanted to control the narrative on the accident, and he did. He controlled every aspect, and with Albert Sanders sent home, the coroner and newspaper reporters were left with only what Ed McDonald told them. We were left with only two choices, believe every word that Mr. McDonald told you, or call into doubt the story. But by handling everything in-house and controlling the narrative of what everyone was told, there was no reports after the fact. There was no charges filed. There was no trial. There was nothing for anyone to question, except the story given to the newspapers. Ingenious.

CHAPTER FOURTEEN
COULD IT HAPPEN TODAY?

If you died on the grounds or in the building of the State Capital today, do you know what agency would investigate? The answer is the Capital Police Department. That is unless they knew that an appearance of impropriety existed, in which case they would ask an outside agency to step in. But it's not mandatory that they do that. Should they choose to keep the investigation in-house, they are within their rights to do so. Many people see the uniformed officers in the Capital building and assume they are security guards, but they are not. Although security is a big part of their job, they are indeed a real police department. They enforce the law inside the Capital and on the grounds of the Capital Complex. It's one of those quirks in law where authority is given to agencies that don't necessarily have a lot of experience in criminal investigation. An example of this is when we see Park Rangers investigation a crime when a body is found on Park grounds. There are certain crimes that should be investigated by trained and better equipped departments than a Park Ranger or Capital Policeman, but laws would have to be changed for that to happen. I certainly do not intend for this to sound like I'm demeaning Park Rangers or Capital Police. I have nothing but respect for both departments and the men and women that serve in those departments. But if myself, or one of my family members turns up dead, these are not the departments I want doing the investigation.

So, if a terrible accident happened today, and you were killed in the Capital building, would the Capital Police do the investigation? Or, would they ask another department to step in and do the investigation? Even today, that's up to them to make the call. It's their jurisdiction and they decide if they or another department will handle the investigation. Once the authorities in the Capital request an outside agency to assist them, the outside agency can decline. This would be a rare occurrence, but due to lack of manpower or conflicts in the agency, they can decline the request to assist. If the Capital Police requested assistance from another agency today, it would most likely be the Arkansas State Police, which is equipped and capable to handle such crime scenes. That would be lucky for us, but in Ira Gurley's day, there was no Arkansas State Police Department. But even if they had existed in 1932, it's very unlikely that they would have been invited to assist.

To answer my own question... "Could this happen today?"... I have to admit that yes it could, even if it's highly unlikely that it would. But then again, it was highly unlikely when it happened to Ira Gurley in 1932.

CHAPTER FIFTEEN
WHAT SHOULD HAVE HAPPENED

I have written about what did happen when the accident occurred, killing Ira Gurley. But what exactly should have happened? Of course, the number one thing that should have NOT happened was Albert Sanders operating the elevator with the door open. But he admitted that he did indeed do this, and a death occurred as a direct result of him doing so. Now's a good time to point out something here. According to Ed McDonald, Albert Sanders admitted to operating the elevator with the door open. Albert didn't admit anything on record, so we have to take Mr. McDonald's word for it. Remember that Ed McDonald sent Albert Sanders home right after speaking to him, so nobody else got the story from Mr. Sanders, only Ed McDonald. Albert Sanders should have been interviewed by Law Enforcement and possibly detained on suspicion of negligent homicide and/or further charges. But that wasn't in the cards being dealt by Ed McDonald. And when the accident happened, should have Albert Sanders pulled the body into the elevator and then transported the body to the basement? Absolutely not! Ira Gurley should not have been moved until emergency personal arrived. The elevator should have been switched off there on the third floor and Ira Gurley kept as still as possible until help arrived. Just like these men not needing law enforcement officers, they seemed to think they could make medical decisions also. Ira had to be near death and dragging him into the elevator and running the elevator down to the basement had to be detrimental, as well as agonizing. Did Albert Sanders think that he was helping by taking Ira to the basement? Or was he following instructions? So many unanswered, and apparently unasked questions. I hate to think about a dying Ira having to endure the four story elevator ride to the basement in that old manually operated 1932 elevator. If there was any conscience activity still in his body, it would have been torture. But I'm sure getting him off of the third floor, in view of the public, was a high priority. After all, the Janitor operating the elevator and killing someone isn't the kind of thing they would have wanted on display in the Capital. That would be too much of an embarrassment during an election year.

Once Albert Sanders had made the mistake of moving the injured body, we need to look at the second blunder in this case. Sending Albert Sanders home! Under no circumstances should this have happened, even if Albert seemed on the brink of collapse, which he did not do. If he was in need of medical attention, he also could have been transported to the hospital. But he wasn't, he was told to go home, which he did without medical assistance. This decision by Ed McDonald is one of the most suspicious points of the incident. Why did Mr. McDonald only want the story to be told by himself, and not the man that actually was in the elevator? Albert Sanders knowing exactly what he was suppose to do after the accident, and Ed McDonald immediately sending him home, raise red flags that should have been explained. But nobody was asking questions.

And this brings us to the third blunder that leaps out at us. One of the Secretary of State employees had just killed a man that was intending to run for Secretary of State. Someone not wanting to control the narrative, and whom did not have any motives, would easily have seen that the Secretary of State himself investigating this accident was a conflict of interest. Ed McDonald taking over the accident investigation had appearance of impropriety written all over it. But none of that mattered to Mr. McDonald, he wanted full control, and he had it. If doing the right thing had mattered, a phone call to either the Little Rock Police Department or the Pulaski County Sheriff's Office would have provided the properly trained law enforcement detectives that this incident needed. It's not uncommon for one agency to request the assistance of another agency. As a matter of fact, it's common practice. Particularly if one department wants everyone to know that the investigation is above board and honest. Ed McDonald didn't even have the benefit of a Capital Police Department to assist him. That department had not been formed yet, and even if they had been, they also would have been in-house employee's.

A fourth blunder in the investigation would be not interviewing the two witness's individually. The two ladies that had been on the elevator should have been taken into separate rooms and asked to write down everything about the event that they can remember. But writing statements down were not a part of this investigation, which is outrageous. If the two ladies wrote different stories, that would have brought questions, and if they had both wrote exactly the same thing, that sounds rehearsed. So once again, we have to take someones word on the fact that the two ladies collaborated Albert Sanders story.

Blunder number five is the investigation "team" in this case. The Secretary of State should not have been involved at all, but Ed McDonald was in total control. Guy Amsler being there being represented as someone that sits on the Game and Fish Commission with Ira, which he did, but not one word of him being an attorney is mentioned. He was not there for the benefit of Ira Gurley. And the third member of this team is the Pulaski County Coroner, Dr. Samuel Boyce. He listened to a second party story of what happened and declared the death an accident! Is that even legal? It is if nobody's paying attention or asking questions.

To sum it up in simple terms, this whole accident and investigation was a circus of shambles, jumbles, and disarray. The act of killing a man in the Arkansas State Capital building and writing your own narrative for the investigation was a bold act. But in the case of Ira Gurley, they got away with it. They wrote articles in the newspapers telling Ed McDonald's story of the accident, and that's about all you can find today. No reports in the Secretary of State office, no reports at any police agency, no reports at the Coroners office, and no reports at the Game and Fish Commission. Ira Gurley died on Friday afternoon and on Sunday afternoon they buried him. And the common man in Arkansas went about his business of trying to survive the Great Depression and forgot about the accident. No questions asked.

CHAPTER SIXTEEN
WHAT'S THE POINT NOW AND WHY SHOULD WE CARE?

Ira Gurley is a forgotten man today. No school children learn of him, and no memorials tell of his accomplishments. Now, Ira Gurley is a headstone in the grave yard surrounded by other headstones. His tireless work in the education of the young in the Ozarks now goes without mention. Even at our Historical Museum in Berryville, Arkansas you have to dig to find tidbits about Ira. There's the rare school photo of him teaching in a one room schoolhouse or the mention of his name in a family album. But it's safe to say that the events of that day in 1932 have largely, like Ira himself, been forgotten.

After ninety years, I believe we should remember Ira and his work, not only in the Carroll County schools and churches, but also his work as a State Representative. Perhaps by lowering the State flag to half mast every June 17th, the day of his death, would promote local questions and conversations about Ira each year. This would bring Ira's name to the forefront at least once a year, and keep his memory alive.

I like the idea of people openly discussing Ira and what happened to him. It's a good reminder to us all of what can happen to any of us. One day you're a major player in local or state affairs, and the next day you're forgotten, and all the details of why, get brushed under the rug. I think Ira deserved better.

And what about the other characters from this event? I think Albert Sanders should have been investigated. He should have faced negligent homicide charges, and it should have been made public that he was indeed not the Assistant Elevator Operator, but was in fact the Janitor. Is there means by which we can now his intent that day...Absolutely not. Can we say he killed Ira Gurley on purpose? Absolutely not. But the lack of questions and the cover up of the events also means that we can't positively believe the story that was told. All we're suppose to know about Mr. Sanders is that he was filling in for the regular Elevator Operator, he was running the elevator with the door open, and when Ira Gurley was crushed in the door frame of the elevator, Albert was so upset he had to be sent home. And that's the end of the story, unless you dare question the story, which at the time, nobody did.

The hardest character in this drama to figure out their motives is Secretary of State Ed McDonald. Can any proof be shown that he knew ahead of time that an accident was planned? Absolutely not. Is there any proof that he covered up the facts to save face for his office during an election year? That point is certainly worth debate. Can we say that Ed McDonald had Ira Gurley killed? Absolutely can't be proven. This entire book is based on the fact that Mr. McDonald set up a huge smoke screen around this accident, and personally saw to it that no law enforcement agency was involved. He wasn't truthful about what Mr. Sanders job was, and he sent him home, preventing him from telling his story to anyone else. Maybe, and this is just another scenario, Ed McDonald was protecting a loyal employee. Like everything else in this accident, we just do not know for sure.

What about the Governor and other elected officials? Should we be upset that they didn't step in and demand that Ed McDonald step aside and let another agency handle the investigation? I say yes, but the era of the times, and the "bond" of a one party system, demanded that everyone look the other way. Speaking negatively of another member of your own political party, unless you're in a primary race, is frowned upon by both parties and not often seen. And everyone sitting in elected office during 1932 were Democrats. No opposition voice could be found. So the elected officials of the day staying mum and not questioning events is really no surprise to anyone.

I want to mention the two witnesses to the accident. The two ladies that we're told collaborated Albert Sanders story. What they actually said was...(1)... Ira was standing in front of the elevator door. (2)... Ira stepped aside to allow them off the elevator. (3)...The elevator started immediately after they stepped out. (4)... Ira darted by them to enter the elevator. End of story. They saw nothing after that. They did not see Ira jumping onto the elevator. They did not see Albert sliding the cage door into Ira and pinning him in the doorway. According to their story, they did not see Ira being crushed. Both ladies told the exact same story, which is surprising when you consider how manic and hectic this event must have been. Wasn't it? Wouldn't one think that when this accident happened, there must have been screams, yells, panic, calls for help, people rushing to see what the screaming was about. But we're told that the ladies saw and heard nothing and just kept walking. Albert calmly stopped the elevator and pulled Ira inside and took the elevator to the basement. That just doesn't make sense and is a real sticking point with me. I think both of these ladies were innocent bystanders, and in no way a part of a plot to do wrong. Just two ladies in the wrong place at the wrong time. It's hard to say they were coached on what to say, and under normal circumstances I would believe their story, but there was nothing normal about this accident. I believe sense we didn't get a proper investigation that it's possible they were repeating a story that they were told to tell. Is it at least a possibility?... Yes.

While the reader is reading this book, it's hard to put oneself into the times that these events happened. We're sitting in our comfortable surroundings and can't imagine this happening to anyone we know. Especially inside of our State Capital building! But, when you study the times, the Depression, the one Party System of government, the presence of criminal element, (Mob), in the State, and the day to day struggle of the everyday men and women of the era, maybe what happened isn't so surprising. There's always going to be someone around that would take advantage of your trust. Even in the world we live in today.

CHAPTER SEVENTEEN
THE RESEARCH AND INSPIRATION

As a Historian and Board Officer at the Historical Museum in Carroll County, I've researched thousands of stories about the past history of Carroll County and it's people. The county was formed in 1833, which is three years before Arkansas became the 25th State of the Union in 1836. I've read countless interesting stories about the people, the conditions, and their internal fortitude to survive and thrive. Some of the events that happened to the people from our past leaves questions about the true story of what happened to them. But no story that I have researched, has jumped out at me, like the story of Ira Gurley and his death in 1932. I just can't accept the story as told, and therefore felt an obligation and need to expose the story, and explain why I did not accept it.

If people assume that I'm saying Ira Gurley was murdered that day, they would be wrong. I have no proof of a murder. What I am saying, is that the investigation was so obviously tainted, that it is impossible to accept the story as told. And the fact that such pains were taken to keep Law Enforcement Officers out of the investigation, left me with questions on top of questions that can't be answered today. It was so plainly a twisted story that I was left doubting the entire story. If part of the story was misleading, perhaps all of the story is misleading. If a real investigator had been in charge, none of the story told would have been questioned today. We could have assumed that detectives interrogated the witnesses and investigated the scene. But we were left to "just accept as fact what we tell you" as told by Secretary of State Ed McDonald. With the proper investigators on the scene, Ed McDonald isn't even a part of this story, unless something is uncovered during the investigation that incriminates him. But there was no chance of that happening with him running the investigation.

This was a carefully controlled investigation by the one person in the world that should not have been conducting the investigation. Ira Gurley had no voice in this investigation, and his story would forever be silent, unless someone read the story, saw the obvious flaws of the investigation, and decided to pick the story apart, piece by piece, until perhaps an opposing view developed. That is what I have attempted to do with this book. Just to point out the absurdity of accepting the story as told. If this happened today, I like to think that the press would be all over the story. Demands for an outside agency to investigate would be made, and everyone involved would have to account for their actions. But this was Arkansas in 1932, a much different Arkansas than the one we live in today. Arkansas was a poor rural state, Hot Springs, Arkansas was a mobsters playground, and everyday citizens were just trying to survive the Great Depression. There was no accountability.

So I set out to give Ira Gurley a voice in the investigation. I wanted to openly state what might have really happened, but due to no real investigation, we'll never know for sure. Some of the proposed outcomes are harsh and incriminating, but I'm simply stating what we're left to imagine, due to the bumbling of this so called investigation. When someone tries so hard to totally control the narrative, as Ed McDonald did, we have to step back and ask why. So much of this accident, and what we were told, leaves us asking why, and why did nobody ask why in 1932?

So, here I am, ninety years later and I'm asking why. When people today speak about Ira Gurley, I would hope that his accomplishments are remembered. His work in education, his work as an Arkansas State Representative, and his work with the Arkansas Game and Fish Commission. I would hope that people remember him as the father of Helen Gurley Brown. And I hope it's remembered that when he died that day in 1932, nobody spoke for him. The true victim in this accident had no voice. You had Ed McDonald, the man holding the office that Ira Gurley wished to hold, controlling the narrative. The man operating the elevator, Albert Sanders, was immediately sent home. The Coroner, Dr. Samuel Boyce declard the death accidental without even speaking with Albert Sanders. Stop and think about that for just a minute. If you were investigating a death where a man was crushed in an elevator, wouldn't you want to speak to the elevator operator? But we're told he was upset and needed to go home to rest! How does that conversation go? " Gee Albert, you look upset about crushing Ira in the elevator. Why don't you go home and I'll handle everything. Go home, don't worry, see you tomorrow, I got this." Of course, that's probably not exactly how the conversation went, but possibly there are some similarities to the actual conversation. We'll never know.

I know these scenarios seem harsh, but I think a man being crushed to death and then having a flawed investigation is harsher. There's no way to question the events of that day without having harsh thoughts of what might have happened. The characters in this story have no right to be appalled by the questions, since it's their cover up and flawed investigation that caused the questions in the first place. If you don't want to be questioned about intent, actions, and motives, just step aside and let a real detective handle the case. But I can't help thinking there was a reason Ed McDonald wasn't going to allow that to happen. His actions leave me questioning everything.

CHAPTER EIGHTEEN
A BELIEVE IT OR NOT LIST

Since Ed McDonald saw to it that the only story that was shared with the public was his story, let's take his story and the events of the day and see what is believable, and what seems to be not totally true.

1. Ira Gurley shows up for a meeting at the Capital building on the day that the Elevator Operator is given the day off. Coincidence? There is no evidence to indicate that the Janitor operating the elevator the day of the accident was anything other than coincidence. Unless you consider the accident itself as proof.

2. There is also no evidence presented that the meeting Ira was there for had anything to do with the accident. We just don't know.

3. The elevator was being operated by the Assistant Elevator Operator. That one we know is not true. Albert Sanders was a Janitor. And the year before that, he worked as a yardman.

4. The elevator was occupied by two ladies that worked in the Capital Building. There's no reason to doubt this. Were they put on the elevator to supply affirmation to the Albert Sanders story? Probably not, but it's another question that will never be answered. So we're left thinking it's a possibility regardless of how unlikely.

5. Both ladies saw Ira Gurley standing right in front of the elevator when the door opened, but the man operating

the elevator swore he never saw him. Another part of the story that is very hard to believe. Albert Sanders was opening the door and would have had to have had his eyes closed to miss Ira standing right there. And again, did anyone ask if the floor light was on inside the elevator telling the operator that someone was waiting on the elevator on the third floor? Seems no questions were asked, but it's pretty safe to assume that someone waiting on an elevator had pressed the button to notify the operator they were waiting. But the light signaling someone on the third floor waiting and the fact that Ira Gurley was standing right in front of the door somehow still got past Albert Sanders. The ladies stated that Ira had to step sideways to allow them off of the elevator or else they could not have gotten by him.

6. Albert Sanders decided to start the elevator upward without closing the door. What?! Too bad Albert was not asked why, because I'd be interested to know what reason he might come up with. It makes no sense that he did this, and we're left trying to reason why someone would do that. We were given no answers. And the statement that the elevator started upward the second the ladies stepped off is also a clue. The ONE thing that everyone was stressing, (even though none of the statements were rehearsed), is that the elevator started the second the ladies stepped out. The one point that makes the argument for accident and not pre-meditated is the one point everyone stressed. That's just suspicious to me.

7. After starting the elevator upward, Albert slid the cage door closed. Ira, seeing that the elevator was started

upward, darted past the ladies and jumped onto the moving elevator. Still not seeing Ira, Albert pushed the door into Ira's chest and pinned him in the doorway. It doesn't say he hit Ira with the cage door, it doesn't say he bumped Ira with the cage door, it says he penned Ira with the cage door while still claiming he didn't see Ira. And yet, nobody thought any of this needed investigating and nobody needed to be interrogated. They acted as if this was a routine day in the Capital and there's nothing to see here. Just move along. Still believe everything you're being told?

8. Ira was pulled into the elevator by Albert Sanders and taken to the basement where ambulance paramedics took over withing minutes. I'd like a verification of "within minutes." This was 1932 and there was no 911 service in those days. While Ira lay dying on the floor of the elevator, Ed McDonald had been summoned from his office. He took full control of the scene and sent Albert Sanders home. All we know for sure, is that the paramedics pronounced Ira Gurley dead before they reached the hospital.

9. Ed McDonald decides that he will conduct the investigation in-house and there's no reason to call in an outside agency because it's an obvious accident. This would be a huge falsehood. There is plenty of reason to request another agency step in and handle the investigation, unless, you don't want the accident investigated. Ed McDonald didn't want Albert Sanders or the two lady witnesses talking to the Police. Wouldn't it be nice if we knew the reason why.

10. The two ladies on the elevator telling the exact same story
     and nothing added is proof that Albert Sanders was
     telling the truth. Wrong! The fact that both ladies told
     identical stories with no variations gives the impression
     that it's rehearsed. It just sounds too much as if they're
     being told what to say.

11. Asking a member of the Arkansas Game and Fish
     Commission to join in on the investigation proves Ed
     McDonald had nothing to hide. False! There's plenty of
     questions left unanswered in why Guy Amsler was invited
     to join in as Ed McDonald conducted his investigation,
     but a very good guess would be that Ed wanted a lawyer
     there with him for advise. Reading the newspaper articles
     about the accident, it sounds like Guy Amsler was there
     because he was a coworker of Ira Gurley. But Guy was not
     there for Ira.

12. Do I find it strange that the man that held the office that
     Ira Gurley wanted, is the man conducting the
     investigation into his death? Of course! And it's strange
     he's conducting the investigation of an accident involving
     one of his employee's. And then Ed McDonald follows
     the body to Green Forest and somehow gets appointed as
     one of the honorary pallbearers at the funeral. Yes, I find
     it very strange indeed.

13. Do I think it's coincidence that Ira's family left the State
     after his death. Unless they were daring to ask questions,
     they were of no worry to a anyone in the Capital. My best
     guess is that Cleo Gurley was just looking for the best life
     and opportunities for her daughters. Somewhere far away
     from Arkansas and the memories that remained here.

14. Is the silence of the other Government officials in this case surprising? NO, in fact it's par for the course in party politics.

15. Where was the Press? They showed up to cover the story, listened to Ed McDonald tell his story, and then printed the story as told. But I'm surprised not one sharp investigative reporter asked a few questions. If they did, I've never it printed.

CHAPTER NINETEEN
FINAL FRUSTRATION

The final frustration in writing this book is in the knowing that we'll never have the true answers of what happened that day in the Capital. I'll never be able to tell you that I 100% know what happened. Ninety years is a long time to try and uncover facts when they've laid so dormant for so long. If there had been a fender bender on the parking lot, or perhaps a dispute between two separate individuals, it would be easy to see if the matter was handled in-house by the Secretary of State. But that's not what this was, not by a long shot. This was a man being crushed in an elevator and losing his life. A death occurred and it was handled in-house with no Law Enforcement Agency involved.

So I have to wrap this up by saying that after a two year investigation of my own, I can't tell you what happened for sure. I can only tell you that the investigation of 1932 was flawed in many different ways, which I have pointed out in this book. There is no claim here that what they say happened is a lie. I'm saying, "How would we know?"

I hope the family of Ira Gurley is glad that someone finally asked questions that should have been asked ninety years ago. I also hope that this book does not cause further frustration for them. The main person that I wrote this book for was Ira Gurley himself. Ira went to bat for the people of Carroll County through his work in education, law, and politics. It's about time someone went to bat for him.

So even though it's been years since Ira Gurley died, I want to say thank you. Thank you for all you did, and please know that as long as there is a Carroll County Historical & Genealogical Society, you will not be forgotten.

IRA GURLEY DIES IN ELEVATOR MISHAP

Game and Fish Commission Employe Fatally Crushed at Statehouse.

Ira M. Gurley, aged 40, 419 North Monroe street, for the past seven years assistant secretary of the Arkansas Game and Fish Commission, was injured fatally yesterday shortly beore 1 p. m. when he was crushed while attempting to board an elevator in the state capitol building. He died en route to Baptist State hospital in a P. H. Ruebel & Co. ambulance.

Dr. Samuel G. Boyce, coroner, who with Guy Amsler, secretary of the commission, conducted an investigation, held that the death was the result of an accident.

Mr. Gurley was awaiting the elevator on the third floor of the building when the operator, Albert Sanders, 618 Battery street, opened the door. Miss Emma Hill, employed in the state comptroller's office, said that as she left the car, Mr. Gurley stepped aside to permit her to alight. Almost at the same instant, Sanders started the car, pulling the door shut simultaneously. Mr. Gurley stepped onto the floor of the car as it started up.

He was caught between the elevator and the door opening, his head and feet inside the car, his back and hips outside.

Sanders lowered the car to the basement where the ambulance crew took charge of the victim a few minutes after the accident. The operator then was permitted to go home. He was on the verge of a collapse.

Miss Hill's version of the tragedy was corroborated by Miss Etra Lee Jordan, who is employed in the state Health Department.

Sanders, a relief elevator operator, told Ed F. McDonald, secretary of state, that he did not see Mr. Gurley until too late to avoid the accident.

Former Legislator Killed In Accident at Statehouse

IRA M. GURLEY.

North Little Rock

Programs of Sunday Services At Local Churches.

The Rev. Sam B. Wiggins, pastor of the First Methodist church, will use for the subject of his sermon tomorrow morning, "How to Be Happy." At the night service the subject will be

IRA GURLEY DIES IN ELEVATOR MISHAP

Game and Fish Commission Employe Fatally Crushed at Statehouse.

Little Rock, June 18.—Ira M. Gurley, aged 40, 419 North Monroe street, for the past seven years assistant secretary of the Arkansas Game and Fish Commission, was injured fatally Friday shortly before 1 p. m. when he was crushed while attempting to board an elevator in the state capitol building. He died en route to Baptist State Hospital in an ambulance.

Dr. Samuel G. Boyce, coroner, who with Guy Amsler, secretary of the commission, conducted an investigation, held that the death was the result of an accident.

Mr. Gurley was awaiting the elevator on the third floor of the building when the operator, Albert Sanders, opened the door. Miss Emma Hill, employed in the state comptroller's office, said that as she left the car, Mr. Gurley stepped aside to permit her to alight. Almost at the same instant, Sanders started the car, pulling the door shut simultaneously. Mr. Gurley stepped onto the floor of the car as it started up.

He was caught between the elevator and the door opening, his head and feet inside the car, his back and hips outside.

Sanders lowered the car to the basement where the ambulance crew took charge of the victim a few minutes after the accident. The operator then was permitted to go home. He was on the verge of a collapse.

Miss Hill's version of the tragedy was corroborated by Miss Etta Lee Jordan, who is employed in the state health department.

Sanders, a relief elevator operator, told Ed F. McDonald, secretary of state, that he did not see Mr. Gurley until too late to avoid the accident.

Tribute from Official

"Mr. Gurley," Mr. Amsler said, "was a gentleman of fine character and the loss of his services will be keenly felt."

Born October 10, 1891, near Alpena Pass, Boone county, Mr. Gurley attended the public schools of the county and later was graduated from Green Forest High School. In 1916 he was graduated from Cumberland Law School at Lebanon, Tenn. On June 10, 1917, he married Miss Cleo Fred Sisco of near Green Forest. Prior to and after his graduation from law school, Mr. Gurley taught school in Carroll and Boone counties and formerly was principal of the Green Forest High School. He was a member of the Methodist church at Green Forest and served as superintendent of the Sunday school of that church for several years. He was a member of the Modern Woodmen of America.

In 1919 he served as representative from Carroll county. In 1921, 1923 and 1925, he was chief clerk of the House of Representatives. He was employed by the state Game and Fish Commission in June 1925, as assistant secretary and had filled that position since.

Mr. Gurley is survived by his wife, two daughters, Eloise, 13 and Helen Gurley, 10; three brothers, James of Happy, Texas, and H. H. and J. O. of Los Angeles, Calif. and three sisters, Mrs. John McCollum of Dallas, Texas, Mrs. S. F. Maples of Alpena Pass, and Mrs. Bert Plott of Harrison, and his father, J. H. Gurley of Green Forest.

Funeral services were conducted at 2 p. m. Sunday at Green Forest, in charge of the Rev. C. H. Sherman of Mountain Home and the Rev. W. A. Downum of Green Forest, with burial in the Glenwood cemetery at Green Forest. The body was taken by train to Green Forest at 10:30 Saturday night.

Pallbearers were: Active—J. E. Gregson, Luther Owens, J. W. Trimble and Ted Coxsey, Berryville; Ray Anderson, Massey Seitz, Green Forest and W. A. Rooksbery and Guy Amsler, both of Little Rock. Honorary—Henry Wilson and B. O. George, both of Berryville; Harry Neely, Searcy; Judge G. B. Ewing, McGehee; Charles H. Tompkins, Prescott; W. N. Deaton, Conway; C. M. Sisco, Siloam Springs; W. R. Phillips, Elmer Reeves, C. C. O'Neal, W. J. Tate and John Stafford, all of Green Forest; Albert Bell, Frank Whittaker and L. C. Brown, all of Alpena Pass; F. O. Butt and C. A. Fuller, both of Eureka Springs; A. J. Russell, Ed F. McDonald, Lee Miles, Jim R. Higgins, F. A. Rowland, E. I. McKinley, Floyd Sharp, Ed R. Hicks, Jimmy Newcomb, W. H. Mann, H. O. Topf, Ray V. Leonard, Ira C. Sussky, H. C. Gibson, Dr. G. M. Reagen, A. R. Lamb and Judge Turner Butler, all of Little Rock.—Arkansas Gazette.

Injury In Elevator Fatal to Ira Gurley

Green Forest Man, Native Of Boone County, Killed In Capitol Accident.

Little Rock, June 18—Rushing to board an elevator in the capitol building at noon Friday, Ira M. Gurley, 36, assistant secretary of the Arkansas game and fish commission and widely known over the state, was fatally injured when caught between the door and the car. A coroner's investigation held the death the result of an accident.

Gurley, who twice was chief clerk of the lower house of the legislature, died on the way to a hospital. His neck was broken, and his chest was crushed.

The elevator was in charge of Albert Sanders, 50, relief operator, who said he did not see Gurley until the car had moved a few feet upward.

Born October 10, 1891, near Alpena Pass, Boone county, Mr. Gurley attended the public schools of the county and later was graduated from Green Forest High School. Prior to and after his graduation from law school, Mr. Gurley taught school in Carroll and Boone counties.

He is survived by his wife, two daughters, Eloise, 15 and Helen Gurley, 10; three brothers, James of Happy, Tex. and H. H. and J. O. of Los Angeles, Calif., and three sisters, Mrs. John McCollum of Dallas, Texas, Mrs. S. P. Maples of Alpena Pass and Mrs. Bert Plott of Harrison, and his

An order for the veterinarians, who are now testing cattle in Carroll county, to do some check-up work in Benton county will temporarily stop the work in this county.

For this reason, no testing will be carried on in Carroll County during the month of July. Testing will be resumed August 1 in Yocum township and will then be carried on continuously until the entire county has been covered. The next announcement of bunching places will appear in the county agent's notes in this paper about the middle of July. Please watch for it.

Read this weeks advertisements.

IRA GURLEY DIES IN ELEVATOR MISHAP

Game and Fish Commission Employe Fatally Crushed at Statehouse.

Little Rock, June 18.—Ira M. Gurley, aged 40, 410 North Monroe street, for the past seven years assistant secretary of the Arkansas Game and Fish Commission, was injured fatally Friday shortly before 1 p. m. when he was crushed while attempting to board an elevator in the state capitol building. He died en route to Baptist State Hospital in an ambulance.

Dr. Samuel G. Boyce, coroner, who with Guy Amsler, secretary of the commission, conducted an investigation, held that the death was the result of an accident.

Mr. Gurley was awaiting the elevator on the third floor of the building when the operator, Albert Sanders, opened the door. Miss Emma Hill, employed in the state comptroller's office, said that as she left the car, Mr. Gurley stepped aside to permit her to alight. Almost at the same instant, Sanders started the car, pulling the door shut simultaneously. Mr. Gurley stepped onto the floor of the car as it started up.

He was caught between the elevator and the door opening, his head and feet inside the car, his back and hips outside.

Sanders lowered the car to the basement where the ambulance crew took charge of the victim a few minutes after the accident. The operator then was permitted to go home. He was on the verge of a collapse.

Miss Hill's version of the tragedy was corroborated by Miss Etta Lee Jordan, who is employed in the state health department.

Sanders, a relief elevator operator, told Ed F. McDonald, secretary of state, that he did not see Mr. Gurley until too late to avoid "was a gentleman of fine character and the loss of his services will be keenly felt.".

Born October 10, 1891, near Alpena Pass, Boone county, Mr. Gurley attended the public schools of the county and later was graduated from Green Forest High school. In 1916 he was graduated from Cumberland Law School at Lebanon, Tenn. On June 10, 1917, he maried Miss Cleo Fred Sisco of near Green Forest. Prior to and after his graduation from law school, Mr. Gurley taught school in Carroll and Boone counties and formerly was principal of the Green Forest High School. He was a member of the Methodist chuch at Green Forest and served as superintendent of the Sunday school of that church for several years. He was a member of the Modern Woodmen of America.

In 1919 he served as representative from Carroll county. In 1921, 1923 and 1925, he was chief clerk of the House of Representatives. He was employed by the state Game and Fish Commission in June 1925, as assistant secretary and had filled that position since.

Mr. Gurley is survived by his wife, two daughters, Eloise, 15 and Helen Gurley, 10; three brothers, James of Happy, Texas, and H. H. and J. O. of Los Angeles, Calif. and three sisters, Mrs. John McCollum of Dallas, Texas; Mrs. S. F. Maples of Alpena Pass, and Mrs. Bert Plott of Harrison, and his father, J. H. Gurley of Green Forest.

Funeral services were conducted at 2 p. m. Sunday at Green Forest, in charge of the Rev. C. H. Sherman of Mountain Home and the Rev. W. A. Downum of Green Forest, with burial in the Glenwood cemetery at Green Forest. The body was taken by train to Green Forest at 10:30 Saturday night.

Pallbearers were: Active—J. E. Gregson, Luther Owens, J. W. Trimble and Ted Coxsey, Berryville; Ray Anderson, Massey Seitz, Green Forest and W. A. Rockebery and Guy Amsler, both of Little Rock. Honorary—Henry Wilson and H. O. George, both of berryville; Harry Neely, Searcy; Judge G. R. Ewing, McGehee; Charles H. Tompkins, Prescott; W. N. Denton, Conway; C. M. Sisco, Siloam Springs; W. R. Phillips, Elmer Reeves, C. C. O'Neal, W. J. Tate and John Stafford, all of Green Forest; Albert Bell, Frank Whittaker and L. C. Brown, all of Alpena Pass; F. O. Bell and C. A. Fuller, both of Eureka Springs; A. J. Russell, Ed F. McDonald, Lee Miles, Jim B. Higgins, P. A. Rowland, E. I. McKinley, Floyd Sharp, Ed R. Hicks, Jimmy Newcomb, W. H. Mann, H. O. Topf, Roy V. Leonard, Ira C. Sousky, R. C. Gibson

PHOTOS OF DEPRESSION ERA ARKANSAS

"The New Deal" Never
a Step Backward
ARKANSAS
LAN DON
WASHINGTON
ROOSEVELT
ROOSE

Ira Gurley sitting in front middle.

I INCLUDED THESE PHOTOS of Depression Era Arkansas for a reason. Some may read this book and not understand how there was no public uproar. But look again at these photos. The average man in Arkansas had not time for worrying about what was happening in the Capital. They only cared about how they were going to feed their family. So in no way do I hold the general public to blame. They had all of the problems they could handle. On the one hand, you had the average person, that in most cases was a farmer, and he had nothing. On the other hand, you had the criminal element that, with the right bribes, lived the high life in Arkansas. One thing these poor farmers did have was honesty. A man's word was as good as gold. They survived to build the greatest nation in the world. It's a shame that Ira Gurley wasn't there to help them build it.

ABOUT THE AUTHOR
DALE ROSS

Dale and his wife Judith live in Rogers, Arkansas. Both are graduates of Berryville High School in Carroll County. Dale sits on the Board of Directors for the Carroll County Historical and Genealogical Society, and is currently serving as the 2nd Vice President of the Board. Dale created and maintains the Facebook page, "The Carroll County Arkansas History Buffs, " which currently has 4000 members.

In 1999, Dale was hired at the Sherwood Police Department in Sherwood, Arkansas. He served in Dispatch, Detention, Auxiliary Patrol, and Training. It was a remarkable experience where he made lifelong friends and connections. Dale left the police force at the end of 2010. Perhaps one of the biggest lessons learned at the police force was, don't take everything at face value, and don't believe everything you read. That lesson led to the writing of this book.

Dale now assist the Historical Society in maintaining the Carroll County Historical and Genealogical Museum with fundraising and exhibits. He spends many hours each week researching the history of Carroll County and helping to preserve the county's past. Dale has said many times, that the people of Carroll County, Arkansas are the finest and most respectable, honest, and hard working group he has ever known.

Dale and Judith have three grown children, and three grandchildren. The author is an avid Razorbacks fan, and enjoys hiking on the trails in the Ozark Mountains with his wife, Judith.